THIS BOOK
BELONGS TO

_____

A LITTLE GOD TIME

FOR TEACHERS

BroadStreet
PUBLISHING

BroadStreet Publishing Group LLC
Racine, Wisconsin, USA
Broadstreetpublishing.com

A LITTLE GOD TIME FOR TEACHERS

ISBN 978-1-4245-5281-8 (hard cover)
ISBN 978-1-4245-5282-5 (e-book)

Devotional entries composed by Janelle Anthony Breckell, Diane Dahlen, Claire Flores, Rachel
Flores, Deb Perreault, Brenda Scott, Jacquelyn Senske, Christina Sluka, and Carole Smith.

Design by Chris Garborg | garborgdesign.com
Edited and compiled by Michelle Winger | literallyprecise.com

Printed in China.

16 17 18 19 20 21 22   7 6 5 4 3 2 1

LET'S NOT GET TIRED OF
DOING WHAT IS GOOD.
AT JUST THE RIGHT TIME
WE WILL REAP A HARVEST
OF BLESSING IF WE
DON'T GIVE UP.

GALATIANS 6:9

INTRODUCTION

Whether your classroom is in a traditional school building or right next to your kitchen, you face your own set of teaching challenges each day. These daily devotions are written specifically with you in mind. Encouraging words, uplifting Scriptures, and personalized prayers will help spur you on as you continue to deposit wisdom in lives of your students.

Rest assured that your hard work does not go unnoticed. The effort you put into equipping these children now will reap a harvest in years to come.

JANUARY

His divine power has granted to
us everything pertaining to life
and godliness, through the true
knowledge of Him who called us by
His own glory and excellence.

2 PETER 1:3 NASB

RUNNING AHEAD

Humble yourselves under the mighty power of God,
and at the right time he will lift you up in honor.
1 PETER 5:6 NLT

You have a vision for the future and a goal you want to achieve, but you just aren't sure how or when. Once a promise is given, and the goal set, you might find yourself getting anxious. When you have set your hope on the goal being instant, the reality that it isn't hits you hard.

It's easier to run ahead of God than to wait. We become goal oriented, pushing for the vision no matter what. But God's timing is perfect. When you do things on God's timetable, you can step back at the end of it and recognize that he truly did know best. In retrospect, you recognize that all those little setbacks were actually your victories. God perfectly orchestrates his plan. When you humble yourself and trust him to do it, you will be lifted up in a way that is greater than what you first imagined.

Father, help me to trust your plans for my future and to learn your timetable. I don't want to run ahead of you, I want to be led by you. I want to walk with you because I want to be where you are. Give me the patience and the trust required to live according to your plan.

KINGDOM LIVING

He will give eternal life to those who keep on doing good, seeking after the glory and honor and immortality that God offers.

ROMANS 2:7 NLT

Every day you are given two ways in which to walk. God offers you his way and the world offers another. As we grow in our faith, we become more aware of the contrast between the principles of the kingdom of God and the systems of the world. Scripture says that it is better to give than receive and that we should turn the other cheek when we are wronged. It takes a careful examination of our actions to see if we are allowing these kingdom principles to shape our lives.

The world offers us glory through feeding our pride, and honor in the shallow ringing of man's applause. Modern societies strive toward immortality through glorifying youth and fixating on leaving a mark on the world. The glory and honor that the world offers, ironically, will be destroyed. God's Word is the only truth that can promise an eternal reward. Jesus Christ conquered death and promises us that same power as we follow him into eternity. Praise God that his gifts are trustworthy and solid!

Jesus, give me the wisdom to recognize when I am seeking the glory and honor of this world, rather than seeking your kingdom. Thank you that your way is the way of eternal life.

A DEEPER KNOWLEDGE

May God give you more and more grace and peace as you grow in your knowledge of God and Jesus our Lord.

2 PETER 1:2 NLT

The fear of failure is one of life's biggest struggles. Failure is not a great feeling, and yet most successful people will tell you that failure has been a part of their experience as well. There is something to be said for the knowledge that comes from experience. As your experience of God grows, your understanding of simple concepts like peace and grace will develop into deep truths.

The knowledge of God is not a test that you can fail. Every new thing you learn about Christ will add to your faith. Climb the mountains of life with him, test him at his Word, and find his promises to be true. As you explore the truth, your preconceived notions of peace and grace may challenge you. Treasure this deeper understanding in your heart. He will show you the purest forms of the most wonderful things. Invite God to reveal himself to you daily, and experience the joy of discovering a life of fullness in him.

Jesus, I want to know you in a deeper way. I ask you to reveal something of yourself to me today so I can be encouraged with a fresh understanding of your grace and peace.

STAY TRUE

Make every effort to give yourself to God as the kind of person he will approve. Be a worker who is not ashamed and who uses the true teaching in the right way.
2 TIMOTHY 2:15 NCV

Teachers, lecturers, and tutors are trained to know the requirements of writing an academic paper. Sources must be cited appropriately and careful attention needs to be taken to avoid plagiarism. This can be a time consuming process, but it is the expected standard of excellence in academia.

We are warned in the Bible that there will be many false teachers in the last days. Treat the Bible and teachings on God's Word with the same care that you expect from your students' papers. Look for fake gospels by knowing the true source. Consider what you hear and compare it with the Scriptures. Do those you follow have character qualities that are Christ-like, showing the fruit of the Spirit and living a lifestyle that points you to Christ? We can easily be led astray if we are not familiar with the gospel ourselves. Ask God to give you discernment and insight so that you can stay true to his Word and succeed.

Your Word is true and excellent, Lord. Help me not to be led astray by false teachers but discern the truth and walk in it.

A LOVING GAZE

There is no fear in love. But perfect love drives out fear,
because fear has to do with punishment. The one who
fears is not made perfect in love.

1 JOHN 4:18 NIV

She could describe exactly what his eyes looked like, where every fleck and freckle rested, and the direction of every crease. Ask her, however, about the barista that served her coffee or the lady who cut her hair, and it would be a gambler's chance at her ability to get their eye color right. A quick glance is never enough to remember the details. The one she loved was where her gaze lingered. Her time and energy was for those eyes alone.

Jesus is gazing at you with the most complete, overwhelming love in his eyes. We spend a lot of our lives glancing at fear. Our worries and insecurities call out and we look one way and then the other. Quiet your heart today and gaze into the loving eyes of Jesus, recognizing the perfect love he has for you. The fear will subside.

I've been so distracted by fears and worries, Jesus. Look me in the eyes and tell me of your love. Let me sing your praises and drink deeply of the love you have for me today.

CLEAR VISION

The precepts of the Lord are right,
giving joy to the heart.
The commands of the Lord are radiant,
giving light to the eyes.

PSALM 19:8 NIV

Do you remember reading a book as a child near bedtime, and as dusk set in, your mother called out to turn the light on because you were straining your eyes? Perhaps recently you had to get glasses because the road signs had become fuzzy. Once that light came on or those glasses were perched on your face, there was a moment of relief. Things became clearer.

At times, our spiritual life needs this kind of attention. When life gets out of focus or things get too dim, we need to turn a light on. We need to turn to the Lord to bring things back into alignment again. It isn't always a major sin issue or crisis that causes our lives to get out of line. Business, monotonous tasks, and minor distractions can all skew our vision little by little. Ask the Lord to search your heart and see if you need an adjustment today.

Lord, I love your Word! Renew in me a spirit of hunger for your Word, and align my life with it. Show me what things need clarity so I can draw closer to you.

EVERYDAY GRATEFULNESS

Walk in Him, having been firmly rooted and now being
built up in Him and established in your faith, just as you
were instructed, and overflowing with gratitude.

COLOSSIANS 2:7 NASB

When you first came to know Christ, you may have come
to him with all sorts of sin issues—the same things that Paul
addresses when he writes to the Colossian church—greed,
sexual sins, lying, slander, and rage were just a few on his list.
Once you began to grow in your relationship with Christ, you
began to grow in other areas, and sin is replaced with love,
joy, patience, compassion, prayer, and thankfulness. With roots
deeply entrenched in Christ, you will begin to see this fruit
come to maturity in your life.

A key shift for you may be in the discipline of being
thankful. Try to make a habit of writing down something
you are thankful for every day: flowers after a long winter, a
homemade gift from a student, a close parking space, a nice
cup of tea! All of these little blessings will add up to fill your
heart with encouragement and gratitude.

Thank you, Jesus, for setting me free from my sin and
leading me into a maturity that comes from knowing you.
I pray others would see the change in my life that comes
from a heart that is overflowing with gratitude for what you
have done.

REFLECTING HIS WAYS

O God, you have taught me from my earliest childhood,
and I constantly tell others about the wonderful things
you do.

PSALM 71:17 NLT

Little kids find great fascination in clomping around in
their parents' shoes. They imitate what they see around them,
from physical appearance to words and actions. This can be
unnerving when you realize the impression you can make on
the children or students in your life. They may see the good,
but they will also witness the mistakes.

With grace, you can actively model faith to the little ones
around you. Let them see you pray, study Scripture, and cry out
to Jesus. Let them see you worship in dance and praise to God.
The changed life that God has given you will shine brighter than
the mistakes, because even your mistakes can be used for glory
when you demonstrate repentance. Let them see those hidden
things so they can reflect Jesus just as you do.

Jesus, thank you for forgiveness! Thank you for the
brightness of repentance. I pray those around me will see
your power working in my life for your glory.

STUBBORNLY REDEEMED

Therefore, my dear brothers and sisters, stand firm.
Let nothing move you.
1 CORINTHIANS 15:58 NIV

No one enjoys teaching a stubborn child. But stubbornness redeemed is commitment. In our lives, we can be like stubborn children, opposing the will of God and demanding our own way. But we can also be redeemed—stubbornly devoted to following God and keeping our eyes from distractions along the way.

In the lives of our students, we may be the last ones standing in defense against the enemy's plans. We need to be stubborn in prayer, standing firm even when we are last, even when no one notices, even when we can't see the results. Maybe you feel fatigued and battle weary today, or very alone in your stand. Maybe you are tired of being stubborn and want to be stubbornly redeemed. Pray for refreshment and seek out someone who will stand alongside you. Be encouraged that Jesus is the one who brings strength when you need it most.

Jesus, thank you for standing beside me. Please bring brothers and sisters in Christ alongside me in this battle. Let me be stubbornly redeemed for your cause.

1/64TH

"If you have faith like a grain of mustard seed, you will say to this mountain, 'move from here to there,' and it will move, and nothing will be impossible for you.
MATTHEW 17:20 ESV

The height of the tallest mountain in the world is 29,029 feet. Many have seen it, few have scaled it, but everyone knows its name. 1/64th of an inch is the average size of a mustard seed. Which of these things do people write books about, take pictures of, and aspire to go see in their lifetime? But 1/64th of an inch is all you need.

Sometimes we are looking for greatness, for the opportunity to make a big bold move so we appear like we are changing the world. But greatness is not what Jesus needs to make the impossible possible. Jesus requires a mustard seed of faith. *Impossible* looms all around us. At work you may have a student who has been given this title. Maybe your entire classroom should have the label on the door. Perhaps you are facing a sickness that doesn't seem to have an end. Whatever your impossible is, find your 1/64th of an inch! What amount of faith can you stir up in your heart? Find it, and watch God move through you to bring that mountain down.

Dear God, help me find that little bit of faith that I need to move toward your awesome plan for my life! Thank you for making all things possible through you.

THE BEST DEFENSE

If God is for us, who can be against us?

ROMANS 8:31 ESV

It is a timeless tale of older and younger siblings: at home wars may be waged, but at school they become each other's greatest defenders. When a child starts school for the first time, they tend to have much more confidence if they know their older sibling will be around.

To accept something means to receive it. God has received you into his family and he is on your side. When the bullies come out, he is behind you 100 percent. We know that the enemy works against us because we stand with God. Whatever comes your way will fall under the shadow of the one who stands behind you. Your enemy will be totally eclipsed. Let God fight your battles and be your defender, and you will have nothing to fear.

Thank you, God, for welcoming me into your family and treating me like one of your own. Help me to walk in confidence, knowing that you are on my side as my defender and strength.

COUNT TO TEN

Everyone should be quick to listen, slow to speak and slow to become angry, because human anger does not produce the righteousness that God desires.

JAMES 1:19-20 NIV

Anger is like a lion, roaring and thrashing about. It can often come out of nowhere. Think back to a time when you spoke too quickly and damaged or lost a friendship, or perhaps put a project in jeopardy. Anger can eat us up. We breathe more quickly, adrenaline pumps through our veins, our heads pound, and our stomachs hurt. If we allow ourselves to act in anger, we usually end up doing something we regret. Mother's advice to count to ten before speaking is still good. This is God's advice to us as well, that we give our emotions time to settle.

Our anger can mask our ability to understand the truth. If we can tame our anger, we will find that we are in a better place to listen to the other side of the story. Taking the time to listen to others makes it easier for us to respectfully answer them. Remember that the Lord is patient with you. Ask him for the grace that you need to stay calm.

Lord God, soften my heart. Give me a spirit of peace and calm. Help me to listen to those around me, to be slow to anger, and to be a peacemaker in my classroom.

ISLAND OF TRANQUILITY

Whoever is slow to anger has great understanding,
but he who has a hasty temper exalts folly.
PROVERBS 14:29 ESV

No one likes to look foolish, especially in the eyes of the student. We've all seen the teacher who blows up, yelling and demanding silence in a noisy classroom. First, the students cower, and then, with heads down, they cover their faces as they giggle and snort. What was meant to be chastisement turns to folly because the instructor lost control. In this chaotic environment, little learning can take place.

A good teacher knows how to hold back anger, take a breath, or whatever it takes to keep irritation from turning to rage. Their classroom is an island of tranquility, a place of encouragement. Ask the Lord to give you wisdom and grace in those times when you begin to feel out of control.

Dear Lord, I want to be a respected teacher. Help me to curb my temper, and not just react to difficult situations that I encounter. Search my heart and show me my failings that I may grow in love.

KEEP IT IN CHECK

Do not be overcome by evil, but overcome evil with good.
ROMANS 12:21 ESV

When we are frustrated and trying to force conformity in the classroom, we grow angry and sometimes raise our voices. But what do we accomplish? In the short run, we may get the children to obey the rules; but in the long run, after each occurrence, the desire of the students to please and respect the teacher is damaged and reduced. Children can lose their attentiveness, their initiative, and their joy. Even though a loud voice may seem to get the attention of your classroom, it can undermine what you are actually trying to do.

The Bible says to overcome evil with good. When the class is out of control, overcome the negative with positive. Tell a joke or speak very softly. Try something out of the ordinary. Distract the students just for a moment. You will need to rely on your helper, the Holy Spirit, for self-control and grace. Rest assured that ultimately, love wins.

God, help me keep my voice modulated in class. Help me to be slow to anger. I want to seek out ways to overcome frustration and aggravation so give me peace and a sense of calm. Remind me to pray for my students, especially the more difficult ones!

CALM IN CALAMITY

"Let not your heart be troubled. You are trusting God,
now trust in me."
JOHN 14:1 TLB

Everyone has days of apprehension, worry, and fear. There are days that haven't gone according to plan. The students are restless, the lesson plans have been thrown out the window, or perhaps a colleague has challenged your abilities.

Calm yourself by digging deeply into the promises of God. Trusting him with your questions, problems, and worries will cause restfulness in your soul. Be assured that he wants you to be successful. He desires the best for you and your students.

God, thank you for your love and concern. Help me to trust in you each day. Please banish my worries and anxieties. Give me the assurance that you will provide me with the knowledge and assistance that I need each day to do the job you have given me.

GODLY LIVING IS BLESSED LIVING

"Even more blessed are all who hear the Word of God and put it into practice."
LUKE 11:28 TLB

Each day our lives are filled with blessings, though we often don't discern them. Did you notice that cup of robust, aromatic coffee? Did you observe those sweet primroses and daffodils on the drive to work? Your car probably started this morning. There are also those who work behind the scenes to make your classroom the haven it is: the janitor, the hall monitors, or the school secretary. Each one of them has blessed your life at one time or another.

Be encouraged that you are a blessing in the lives of your students! You may be the only friendly face they see all day. While you may or may not be able to quote Scripture, your life is an example of God's Word and can be a blessing and encouragement to those you serve.

Lord God, please make me a blessing to those around me. Help me to discern their needs and to respond with your wisdom. Make me more aware of the small blessings you put in my life each day.

ATTEND TO THE NEEDS

*Do not merely look out for your own personal interests,
but also for the interests of others.*

PHILIPPIANS 2:4 NASB

Jen was a fifth grade teacher in a small, poor school district just outside Sacramento. Most paydays Jen shopped at thrift stores looking for children's shoes, jackets, and sweaters. She found the best deals on extra school supplies. When one boy was absent for several days because he didn't have any shoes to wear to school, she bought him some. The lunches she took to school each day filled a hamper. She'd set up a picnic lunch and share it with her students. "Just taste this," she'd say. "Do you think it needs more mayonnaise?" Never was a child perceived as needy; Jen made out they were doing her a favor.

Jen was a single mother of two boys. Money was often tight, but she found ways to stretch it out to help her students. This is a powerful example of being Jesus to a world full of needs. Are you able to see the needs of those around you and put your own interests aside for the sake of others?

God, make me generous of heart. Help me learn to share what I have with others. Open my eyes to those around me and make me a blessing to them. Keep me aware of the needs of others and help me to make a difference in their lives.

PROFITABLE OBEDIENCE

Commit everything you do to the Lord.
Trust him, and he will help you.
PSALM 37:5 NLT

The disciples were mostly skilled fishermen. In John 21, some of them had fished all night and caught absolutely nothing. They must have been tired, achy, and discouraged. As they began to row their boat toward the shore, they saw Jesus standing on the beach. He asked if they had caught anything for breakfast. Imagine having to tell Jesus that you'd been out all night without any nibbles. Fishing is your vocation! Jesus then tells them to throw their nets over the right side of the boat. It sounds pretty foolish, doesn't it? But these devoted men did what Jesus asked and immediately their nets were full. *Immediately!* They trusted what Jesus had instructed them to do.

There will be times when you feel like your teaching has become unproductive and useless. You have stayed up night after night and don't seem to be getting results. Come back to the shore, where Jesus is standing, and ask for his advice. Can you listen to what Jesus is telling you to do? Trust him; be committed to his Word, and he will help you turn things around.

God, I want to trust you more. I want to be committed to you and your Word. Help me to entrust you with my needs. Let me listen to you as I read your Word.

ASK FOR HELP

We can confidently say, "The Lord is my helper;
I will not fear; what can man do to me?"
HEBREWS 13:6 ESV

Discouragement and worry come upon all of us from time to time. It may seem that nothing is going well. One student has defied your authority. Another just can't seem to understand the concept you've been presenting all week. Perhaps a supervisor has questioned one of your decisions. Maybe you are battling an ongoing health problem. What we do in this time of despair is an indicator of our simple faith. We turn to God, calling upon his name and asking for his help.

The Bible tells us that God will help us in our time of need. He delights in sending you help. He will lift your burden of worry and care. He will show you a situation differently or provide you with a way around a problem. Keeping this promise of God in your heart can supply you with confidence to see the day through.

God, sometimes I struggle with discouragement and worry. I need confidence to know that you will help me in all areas of my life. Help me to call upon you for assistance when I am in need. Take away any fears I have and give me joy.

BY YOUR SIDE

Even when I walk through the darkest valley,
I will not be afraid, for you are close beside me.
Your rod and your staff protect and comfort me.

PSALM 23:4 NLT

Picture walking along a road on a dark night. Eerie, sparkling eyes peek out from the brush on each side of the road. Strange animals growl and the occasional bird shrieks. It's hard to see more than a few feet ahead. You have every reason to be shivering with fear, hesitantly putting one foot in front of the other. You can palpably feel the terror.

Now think of the same scene. The animals are still there, no moon or stars light the way, but something is very different! You skip and sing happily as you make your way down the road. What is different? You are holding onto your Daddy's hand, safe in the knowledge that he will protect you. Know that he is close by today and let it be the encouragement you need to move forward.

God, there are times when I lack courage to face what is going on around me. Take the fears from my heart, walk alongside me, and ward off any dangers that come my way. Remind me that you are my protective Father and will keep me from evil. Thank you for loving me.

KALEIDOSCOPE

You created my inmost being;
you knit me together in my mother's womb.
I praise you because I am fearfully and wonderfully made;
your works are wonderful, I know that full well.

PSALM 139:13-14 NIV

A woman was given a box full of fabric scraps. It was quite a hodgepodge. There was blue and pink, deep gold and yellow, the softest green, and vibrant red. Some of the material had patterns on it. There were chickens and coffee beans and birds and roses, even butterflies. She set about cutting each piece of cloth. First, she cut some into triangles, then some into squares. Taking up her needle, she began to sew the pieces together. A blue triangle next to a red square. Then a green shape next to an orange one. Little by little, the quilt grew. She stitched the quilt together until a beautiful kaleidoscope of shapes and colors swirled around the covering. She had created a beautiful thing from a mishmash of cast-off scraps.

Your classroom can be like that quilt. Each student is different, their needs and personalities unlike the one sitting next to them. But with care and creativity, you can help them become who they are meant to be.

Lord God, your creativity amazes me. I thank you that you made me unique and special. Give me the eyes of an artist to see the beauty in my students. I want to help them make the most of their potential.

DISCOVERING BEAUTY

The whole earth is filled with awe at your wonders.
PSALM 65:8 NIV

Have you ever looked at a spider's web covered with dewdrops? What about the iridescence of a hummingbird wing, a glistening canyon covered in ferns, a breathtaking sunset, or a chubby-faced giggling baby? Our hearts soar overlooking the snowcapped mountains and listening to birdsongs on a summer's afternoon.

Each day we are presented with the beauty of God's world. This includes the people he has put under our care. Beauty can be seen in the little girl with a darling lisp as well as the pierced and tattooed teen with purple hair and attitude. It emanates from the students who are eager to learn as well as the problem kids who sit in the back of the class. They are all wonders of God's creation. Sometimes we need to slow down a bit to look for the beauty and diversity of the world around us. You may be surprised to find it on your daily drive or by listening a little closer to one of your students.

Lord God, help me to see the world around me with new eyes of amazement. I am in awe of your wonders. I want to see and appreciate the miracles you have placed right in front of me.

IT IS WORTH IT

Let us not get tired of doing what is right,
for after a while we will reap a harvest of blessing.
GALATIANS 6:9 TLB

Teaching is hard work: lesson plans, classroom prep, bulletin boards, field trips, staff meetings, and grading papers. These tasks are quite time consuming and we haven't even mentioned actual time in the class! Is it worth it? Yes! Sometimes there is an immediate gleam in the eye of a child who understands the new concept you present and sometimes it is not until years later that the kernel of wisdom germinates and blossoms.

It is easy to be discouraged if you see no progress in your classroom. But improvement will come. You have been well trained to do your job. You have many resources to call upon. Ask God for wisdom; go to his Word. A change for the better is right around the corner.

God, sometimes it's easy to get into a rut. Help me to see the wonders around me and to remember that each day is new. Even if I can't see progress, you are working each moment toward blessing. Give me the energy to keep up the good work!

HONEYCOMB

Pleasant words are like a honeycomb,
sweetness to the soul and health to the bones.
PROVERBS 16:24 NKJV

The writer of Proverbs understood honeycomb as "health to the bones." Scientists have now discovered eating honeycomb can lower bad cholesterol and raise the good cholesterol in our bloodstreams. The antioxidants found in the comb can protect liver function and even lower insulin levels in the body.

Just like sweet honey, encouraging and supportive words can make anyone soar. Endorphins are released into the brain, self-esteem is raised, and a general feeling of euphoria can be realized. Conversely, sour or angry words can do more than just hurt feelings. Teachers are sometimes called to be cheerleaders. Encouraging your students to learn, to try again, and to push toward a goal is beneficial to their soul.

God, please help me to speak words of encouragement to my students. May I foster a classroom atmosphere of positivity instead of negativity. Give me patience to keep my temper and help me to seek out the good in each of my charges.

A LIFETIME OF INFLUENCE

Surely goodness and mercy shall follow me
all the days of my life,
and I shall dwell in the house of the LORD forever.
PSALM 23:6 ESV

How many students does a teacher influence in their lifetime? Elementary teachers will have twenty to thirty boys and girls each year. Middle school and high school teachers will have four or five times as many. At the very least, it could be over twelve hundred students in a forty or forty-five year teaching career. Imagine!

You can make a lasting difference in the lives of so many. You can influence each and every one of these children by what you say and how you conduct yourself. Your example may determine where they spend eternity.

Dear God, help me to be a positive impact on the lives of my students. I want a seed I plant in their lives to grow to fruition. My wish is that all of them would spend eternity in your house. Show me how to guide them on their way.

GODLY ACCOLADES

Whatever you do, work at it with all your heart,
as working for the Lord.

COLOSSIANS 3:23 NIV

Each year there are teachers singled out for distinction. The awards may be for Teacher of the Year, Educators of Distinction, an honor society of some kind, or another medal or decoration. These instructors are highly praised for their teaching techniques, their work among special needs children, or their ability to encourage a higher percentage of students on to college. Maybe they wrote a textbook, suggested a new curriculum, or helped their school secure grant funds for a new project.

You should never be discouraged if you are not the one to receive such accolades. To be a teacher of excellence, God requires you to do your best. Take that extra moment to help Mary with her project, pay special attention to those homework assignments, and remind Jordan for the third time to pay attention, without getting frustrated. God has called you to teach; what better distinction is there? Your occupation is important, your students are significant, and you are working to equip the future!

God, I want to find my accolades in you. Make my classroom a place of excellence in learning. Melt my heart for those in my care. Help me to look for opportunities to improve my teaching.

DEAL WITH THE APPEAL

God is faithful. He will not allow the temptation to be more
than you can stand. When you are tempted, he will show
you a way out so that you can endure.
1 CORINTHIANS 10:13 NLT

Ah, temptation...what form of it appeals to you? Is it a
second piece of chocolate cake, too much time on Facebook,
another glass of wine, or just another TV show? It could be
gossiping about the new superintendent, exaggerating the
story you heard at the gym, or avoiding the laundry!

We face all manner of temptations in many situations of
any given day. We know the right thing to do, but it just seems
too hard in the moment to do it. Next time you encounter the
pull of wrong conduct, take a deep breath. Pause and ask God
to deal with the appeal. He will show you what to do. He will
give you the strength to do the right thing. He is faithful to do
it. Every time. He is faithful. Always!

**Dear Lord, show me your faithfulness. Remind me that
you have promised to help me at all times. Keep me from
temptations and show me a way to flee from them. Thank
you for forgiving me when I fail, for picking me up and
setting me on my feet again and again.**

A SOUND MIND

God has not given us a spirit of fear,
but of power and of love and of a sound mind.

2 TIMOTHY 1:7 NKJV

There are many aspects of teaching that cause us to worry. You might have a performance review looming, or a pile of reports on your desk with very little time to finish them. You may be having difficulty understanding a complex problem that you have to explain to your students, tomorrow! Perhaps you are struggling at home because your work-life balance is off kilter. What can you do to relieve yourself of these very real pressures?

The Lord wants the very best for us. Apprehension and fear have no place in our thoughts because they don't come from God. Call on the Holy Spirit to protect you and banish panic and anxiety from your mind. Allow his love and power to reassure you that he has given you a sound mind, full of godly wisdom that will help you deal with every situation.

Dear God, thank you for the love you give me. Help me to seek your power when fear and apprehension find me. Clear my mind of dread and remind me of your grace.

YOUR STRONG TOWER

The name of the Lord is a strong tower;
the righteous runs into it and is safe.

PROVERBS 18:10 NASB

On a walk around the block, a small boy sees a huge, barking dog. The boy cowers in terror, cries, and clings to his father. Papa sweeps him up in his arms and tells the little guy that he is safe.

We are just like that child, and God wants us to go to him in times of trouble. Fear, trepidation, and apprehension can all be put on God's shoulders. He will carry that burden and keep us safe. When you find yourself in a fearful situation, ask the Lord to replace your fears with confidence and love. Like any good father, he is faithful to calm your soul.

God, thank you that you are my heavenly Father. Sometimes I am afraid. Please help me to remember that you are right there waiting and wanting to protect me from the troubles around me.

COMFORT AND COURAGE

God is our refuge and strength,
an ever-present help in trouble.

PSALM 46:1-3 NIV

We live in a flawed world. Schools are locked down these days by threats of terrorists, escaped convicts, and other dangers. Some schools have even been the scene of shootings. We see these pictured on the evening news. Teachers conduct emergency drills for earthquakes, tornados, and fires.

Our schools aren't as safe as we would wish, but we shouldn't fear these events. Your faith in God can help keep your heart from the fear of trouble. Should any of these calamities occur, the Lord will give you courage and peace to be the helper and protector of your students.

Lord, sometimes the world is a scary place. Please take my fears and give me comfort and confidence. Help me to learn how to prepare for and respond in the wake of disaster. Remind me to call on you in times of trouble.

ECONOMICS WITH CHRIST

My God will meet all your needs according to the riches of his glory in Christ Jesus.

PHILIPPIANS 4:19 NIV

No one really likes to talk about finances. We seem to think others will judge us by our financial state. If we are wealthy, then we are successful; conversely, if we don't make a lot of money, we are seen as less important than others. What a bunch of hogwash! God says he will meet all of our needs. *All* of our needs. The Bible doesn't say God will give us a lot of money; his promise is to meet our needs.

God knows what you need. His riches are not always tangible things; his riches are the important things. He knows you need love, joy, gentleness, kindness, and peace of mind much more than you need material riches. Trust the Lord to take care of your finances. Look at what is really important and be rich in those things.

Lord God, thank you for my job and what it provides. Help me to be satisfied with my wages and to use them wisely. Allow me to see the glorious blessings you give me. Thank you that you care for me.

FEBRUARY

How great is the goodness you have
stored up for those who fear you.
You lavish it on those
who come to you for protection,
blessing them before the

watching world.

PSALM 31:19 NLT

A YES RESPONSE

The LORD longs to be gracious to you;
therefore he will rise up to show you compassion.
For the LORD is a God of justice.
Blessed are all who wait for him!

ISAIAH 30:18 NIV

We have all been there. A child comes nagging, a fight breaks your concentration, your name is being called over and over, and you just can't finish… and then you snap, responding in a negative, less-than-forgiving, tone. We all know in our hearts that people are more important than any task we have at hand, but communicating that is a different matter.

Isaiah reminds us of a better way—our heavenly Father who responds to us with a "yes!" How beautiful to have a Father who turns his full attention to us with unending kindness! Remember we are called to be like God. How can we start responding with a yes? Allow graciousness to flow out of knowing he is gracious toward you. Ask God to give you a heart full of compassion for others.

God, I choose the highroad of graciousness when it comes to responding to those around me. Thank you that your heart is turned toward me to show compassion. Let that grace overflow from my heart to those around me, so they know the eyes of a kind heavenly Father.

SUCCESSFUL PLANS

The plans of the diligent lead to profit
as surely as haste leads to poverty.
PROVERBS 21:5 NIV

We expect our students to take their time. Whether it's following all the steps of long division or structuring a sentence, we know careful work will be the effort that brings reward. God wants you to know the same is true for you. The after school hours, the late night planning, and the extra effort that you put in will lead to gain, not only in your students' lives but in your own as well. Proverbs continuously contrasts the lives of the righteous and the unrighteous, the promises and warnings. Heed the warning of haste in this verse. Rushing through and taking shortcuts are empty efforts.

Think of it like a garden. The one that walks outside and throws seeds haphazardly toward the ground cannot expect to feed their family without attending to the garden. The one that takes time to prepare the soil, determine the conditions, and understand when to plant will reap a harvest. So take time to plan and then commit the plans to the Lord. He will begin to work patience in you that will profit your life.

Lord, I commit my plans for today into your hands. Correct and guide me in the right way. Grow patience in my heart so I see the reward of diligence in my life and in the lives of others. Help me not to be tempted to rush things, but to listen to your guidance.

RESERVED

When I discovered your words, I devoured them.
They are my joy and my heart's delight,
for I bear your name,
O LORD God of Heaven's Armies.
JEREMIAH 15:16 NLT

If you walk into a high-end restaurant, you will be asked a simple question: "Name?" Who reserved this feast for you? Whose name are you under? In ancient culture, to be called by another's name indicated ownership by that person. Having their name over you said that you were under the authority and protection of the person who held that name.

Spiritually speaking, your reservation has been made. As someone who calls on the name of Jesus and trusts in his sacrifice, you are under his name. The banquet is constantly spread before you. Is your heart hungry for joy? Eat from his Word. Is your soul parched with weariness? Drink from his Word. Wisdom, joy, comfort, and peace; all of these are a four-course meal set out in the banquet of God's Word.

Lord, make your Word into a feast for my heart. I confess sometimes I don't see the feast laid before me; make your Word sweet in my mouth. Thank you for your protection over me, for sealing me with your Holy Spirit and giving me your strength.

EQUAL OPPORTUNITY

"I was hungry, and you fed me. I was thirsty, and you gave me a drink. I was a stranger, and you invited me into your home. I was naked, and you gave me clothing. I was sick, and you cared for me. I was in prison, and you visited me…. I tell you the truth, when you did it to one of the least of these my brothers and sisters, you were doing it to me!"
MATTHEW 25:35-36, 40 NLT

The idea that every human on the planet is equally valuable is an ideal that many societies try to live up to. In our school systems, you find laws and acts to make sure that every student is getting a good opportunity to succeed. Your students may attend a high-income private school or a low-income public school. They may be three of your own flesh-and-blood or thirty of varying race and gender.

Vulnerable, dependent, and inexperienced are all attributes that define a child or student. You may see your friends building success and promotions in the business world, but you are building lives. There is no such thing as being "just" a teacher. Those who do things for the least in this life will inherit the kingdom of God! Every time you serve that preschool snack or welcome a new class of strangers, you are doing kingdom work that brings rewards far greater than any earthly promotion.

Jesus, thank you for creating a compassionate heart in me. Guard me from discouragement and help me to continue to be faithful in the small tasks, knowing that they are great in your kingdom.

SHARED EXPERIENCE

Be my rock of refuge, to which I can always go;
give the command to save me,
for you are my rock and my fortress....
You have been my hope, Sovereign LORD,
my confidence since my youth.

PSALM 71:3, 5 NIV

Experience is sometimes the best of teachers; wouldn't we all agree? You choose your route to work based on experience in traffic. You know your favorite dishes at a restaurant from previous ordering. You use this knowledge to inform yourself and, in some cases, to inform others.

With God, confidence is supported by experience. The more we walk with him, the more we can confidently declare his goodness. What experiences do you have to declare confidently? It may be times of provision, hope in a tough situation, and perhaps the very first time you called him Savior. What is even more beautiful is that we can share our experience with the youth we influence. If you don't feel like an evangelist or a person of influence, take heart. Use your daily experience of God's grace to build a fortress around the young ones so they can also declare their confidence in him.

Thank you, Jesus for our time together today. Remind me of my testimonies that they may shine bright in a dim world. Allow my hope in you to be a firm foundation that I can confidently share with others.

THE RIGHT ARMOR

Be strong in the Lord and in his mighty power. Put on the full armor of God, so that you can take your stand against the devil's schemes.

EPHESIANS 6:10-11 NIV

She is so independent; he is so creative; she is such an organized person; I just love what a powerful speaker he is! Compliments stick with us and they can help build the identity of who we think we are. Sometimes our greatest compliments reflect the armor that we have put on to mask our deepest fears. Mrs. Independent is really afraid of being abandoned. Mr. Creativity feels the pressure to always produce. Mrs. Organized needs to hold all the control. Mr. Speaker doesn't know how to speak genuinely with those closest to him.

The armor of God is all about attributes of truth, righteousness, peace, faith, and salvation. These are not just compliments. Who holds this complete set of armor? Jesus. He is our best defense against the schemes of the devil. Instead of relying on the armor of this world, put on the true armor of God and let him protect you in his mighty power.

Lord, I need protection; not built with my own hands or ideas or the praise of men, but built by you! Protect me from the lies of the enemy; enlighten my eyes to know what they are, and guide me in truth.

VACATION FOR THE SOUL

"Take my yoke upon you, and learn from me.
For I am gentle and lowly in heart and you
will find rest for your souls."
MATTHEW 11:29-30 ESV

The weeks leading up to spring break find us sitting at our desks, dreaming of a soft ocean breeze blowing in our hair and warm sun washing our bodies. Then a student interrupts with a question that brings us back to reality. Whether spring, summer, or Christmas break, some days we find ourselves longing for that vacation. Even the weekend looming ahead on a rough Wednesday morning seems like a great reprieve from life.

While vacations are a means to escape and find rest, they can never truly cure a weary soul. You could be lying on the beaches of Jamaica or freezing in a classroom in midwest America, and your weary soul would be your companion at both. The only vacation destination for a weary soul is in the presence of Jesus. Find him and drink of the living water. Bask in the glory of a holy God. Rest in his arms of perfect love.

I am weary today, Lord! Draw me into your presence, fill me with living water, and wrap me in your arms so I can find true rest for my soul.

QUIET STRENGTH

The meek shall inherit the land and delight themselves in abundant peace.
PSALM 37:11 NIV

Our culture follows the motto "If you've got it, flaunt it!" Riches, beauty, cute kids, good grades, and beautiful vacations are continually posted online. Real-time updates of everyone else's amazing lives can parade around in our mind, causing unrest and discontentment. The Bible talks a lot about meekness; it is not surprising that this is a word we don't hear or understand in our culture.

Meekness means *quiet strength*. It is humility that models the humility of our Savior. God says the meek are those who will have what everyone really desires—delight and abundant peace! True blessing is having the joy of the Lord: a spiritual prosperity incomparable to earthly riches. Take some time today that you might have spent scrolling social media and give it to the Lord. Ask him to reveal areas of your life that are breeding discontentment and pride, and instead seek to model meekness and humility.

Lord, I repent of discontentment that I have allowed to rob me of your peace. Help me to find delight in you, and to quit the comparison game.

A STORY TO THE END

Let perseverance finish its work so that you may be mature and complete, not lacking anything.

JAMES 1:4 NIV

Have you ever tried to read classic literature? The thick books with tiny print reveal stories that are masterfully woven together. Page after page you follow characters through heartache, triumph, injustice, and love. You don't stop at page 255, as the story is just getting started. If you put it down at page 432, the hopelessness of the situation would consume you. By page 720, you are completely invested! Finally, as that last page slips past your fingertips, the resolution has come, the battle won, the story complete.

Our lives are like one of those books. In God's Word, we know that our stories end with victory! Perhaps right now you feel as though you are on page 255 and have no sense of what is ahead. You might be at page 432 and hopelessness is all you are experiencing. Be encouraged that your story will end well; the author has every page planned out for you. Don't put the book down! Keep turning the pages, and be assured that you will enjoy the completeness of a wonderful finish.

Jesus, thank you that you have written my story! I trust in you and your plan. Strengthen me to keep pursuing you when life gets hard.

PATIENCE FOR ALL

Be patient with everyone.
1 Thessalonians 5:14 NLT

When the end of a lesson draws near, you may find yourself calling out short phrases of important things to remember like, "Don't forget the test next week; remember to have your parents sign your permission slip; don't run in the hall!" The end of Thessalonians sounds a little like this. It's as though Paul is running out of room on his paper and calling out everything he can to help the people he is writing to.

Some may love simple phrases like this because they can act as a quick check of whether you are applying a principle to your Christian walk. Others may be a little bothered about the impossibility of such sweeping statements. Be patient with *everyone*? Be patient with those who frustrate your plans or always seem to create conflict? This fruit of the Spirit can be difficult, but be encouraged! The Holy Spirit is full of patience and willing to strengthen you. Whenever you see yourself lacking, or "everyone" is testing your nerves, stop and lean on the Holy Spirit for help.

Lord, without you I am without patience. Holy Spirit, fill me with your fruit. Thank you that you meet all my needs and are there when I call.

LIVING IN THE NOW

I wait for the LORD,
my whole being waits,
and in his word I put my hope.

PSALM 130:5 NIV

Kids can't wait to grow up. Things like career day thrill them because of the excitement of what is to come! Anticipation of things they aren't old enough to do, like drinking coffee and driving cars, dance in their heads. It seems kids have their next birthday planned as soon as the smoke from their current candles rises!

Sometimes we revert to our childhood tendencies. Our eyes become fixated on the next phase like buying a new house, or getting married, or starting a family, or the next work promotion. We want to press the fast forward button. This psalm reminds us that perhaps we need to quit putting all of our efforts into looking beyond the present. When you posture your whole being in a position of looking the wait straight in the eyes, you will find your gaze centered on Jesus. He is fully present and will satisfy you in your current stage. Find his Word as your daily bread for the here and now.

Jesus I set my eyes on you even though it is hard to wait! I trust that you have the perfect timing for my life and pray that you will be the author of my steps.

ACCEPT HELP

Encourage one another daily, as long as it is called today.
HEBREWS 3:13 NIV

Have you ever heard a story where someone has been in line at a drive-thru, coffee shop, or supermarket and been informed by the cashier that someone else has already paid for their purchase? That would certainly make your day, wouldn't it? We would like to be surprised like that once in a while! Consider the situation where you are out to lunch with friends and one person insists on grabbing the check. You really could use a reprieve from spending, but you protest and insist on paying your own way. We appreciate help when it comes out of nowhere, but admitting we need help can hurt our pride.

The next time the offer of help is extended, accept it. It may wound your pride, but vulnerability opens you up to encouragement and healing. You will find yourself blessed in your relationships and life when you learn to say yes to an extended hand. You will also be inspired to do the same! Take a lesson from other generous people and let encouragement flow freely!

Thank you, Jesus, for giving me friends and family. Help me to encourage and love those around me and to be humble to accept when they want to do the same. Thank you that you know how to provide what I need.

A DIFFERENT PAYCHECK

"Whoever wishes to save his life will lose it; but whoever loses his life for My sake will find it. For what will it profit a man if he gains the whole world and forfeits his soul? Or what will a man give in exchange for his soul?"

MATTHEW 16:25-26 NASB

Good education and finance go hand-in-hand. We want our children to have the best education and to thrive in the system, but this comes at a cost. Finance can be a struggle for teachers. All too often the paycheck doesn't match the true value. This can be discouraging!

When discouragement threatens to settle in, take your eyes off the numbers and focus on the words of Scripture. Make out a new paycheck, listing all the things of true value that you have received, including what the kids under your watch are receiving. Are you rich in the kingdom of God? People who show kindness, gentleness, love, endurance, and wisdom have a paycheck that far exceeds any monetary check. The easiest thing to do in pursuing wealth is to lose yourself. In pursuing godliness, you gain wealth in eternity. Keep receiving those checks from the kingdom of God. You are rich indeed.

Keep my eyes focused on the riches that matter, Lord. Let me lose my life so that I can find it in you.

BEING HIS HANDS

He took the children in his arms, put his hands on them, and blessed them.

MARK 10:6 NIV

We use our hands to communicate warmth when we wave hello to a friend. We use our hands to communicate anger when we ball them into fists. We use our hands to show excitement when we clap and gesture wildly. People were shocked when Jesus used his hands to welcome the children. To the people of that day, favor from God was thought to be earned. Adult hands were to be useful to society: to sacrifice, to provide, to work.

Jesus laid out a perfect example when he welcomed the children into his arms. In the same way, Jesus welcomes you as his child. You don't need to strive or earn your way to the front; he greets you with open arms. You may use your arms today to hold little ones, to point to a problem on the board, or to write an encouraging note to a struggling student. Be blessed by being the hands of Christ.

Thank you, Jesus, for making me your hands to bless and love the children around me. Help me to understand your love for me and willingly communicate this love to those in my care.

FUTURE REWARDS

Whatever you do, work heartily, as for the Lord and not for men, knowing that from the Lord you will receive the inheritance as your reward. You are serving the Lord Christ.
COLOSSIANS 3:23-24 ESV

We can come into teaching with such high ideals. Pinterest boards full of creative ideas, visions of hands raised high, "aha!" moments abounding—it's a beautiful picture. Then you hit month eight or year three and the thrill of your teaching degree and acquired job can begin to fade. Every thankless motion becomes a monotonous deposit. It can be disheartening when the majority of what you hear is complaints from students, parents, principals, and co-workers, rather than a deserved "well done."

How do you know if you have truly made the kind of difference that you set out to make in the classroom? How do you feel validated by the effort that you continue to put into your job? Man's praise is a matchstick lit by a blowtorch. God's reward is well-aged wood that keeps our fire burning throughout our teaching careers. In time, you will see the success of your students as their lives have been shaped and formed. Take some time to evaluate from whom you seek out praise, and remind yourself that your future reward comes from the Lord.

Jesus, my reward comes from you. Thank you for blessing me with a job. Remind me that I am serving you and that your approval is more important than man's praise.

SANCTIFIED

If we confess our sins, He is faithful and just to forgive us our sins and to cleanse us from all unrighteousness.
1 JOHN 1:9 ESV

Have you ever had a student who thinks they are more knowledgeable than you? They talk as if they have the encyclopedia on every subject written in their brains. They have all the information. This is sometimes how we can present ourselves as Christians. We can recite the Easter story as we celebrate it year after year. We know the information. The Christian faith, however, is more than just a static story. It is a story of creation's redemption from sin and the ongoing work of the cross in our lives.

Confession should be a daily part of our walk. Confession keeps us on our toes. It reminds us that we need the grace of Jesus in every moment. Sin doesn't need to define us. When guilt comes knocking on our door, we can confess it out loud and acknowledge God's faithfulness to forgive and cleanse us. We are clothed in righteousness. Who wouldn't want to get dressed in that every morning? Take some time to pause and remember the cross. Remember when you first came to salvation, and thank God for the ongoing work of sanctification in your life. Thank him for his faithfulness.

Jesus, I bring my sin before you and confess that I was wrong. I ask for strength to turn and run the opposite way. Thank you for your forgiveness and love toward me.

CALL TO SERVE

We who are strong must be considerate of those who are sensitive about things like this. We must not just please ourselves. We should help others do what is right and build them up in the Lord. For even Christ didn't live to please himself.

ROMANS 15:1-3 NLT

Every good parent wants the best for their child. They will go the extra mile to make sure their kids succeed at everything from eating to playing instruments. They want them to be healthy, strong, safe, intelligent, artistic, athletic, witty, pretty, fashionable, talented, and everything in between. A parent's world can shrink exponentially when those little bundles first make their appearance in the world.

As a teacher, you have a lot of other people's kids in your care every day! You couldn't possibly treat each child with the same amount of care. Jesus waded into the mess and got right to work. He took off his cloak and started washing feet. He used his strength to serve. You don't have to parent everyone's children, but you can exhibit a Christ-like nature by serving while they are under your care. Ask God to renew your servant heart and let yourself be built up knowing that you are following in the footsteps of your Savior.

Thank you, Jesus, for calling me to be a teacher and for creating a servant's heart in me. Thank you for being the perfect example of what it means to teach, lead, and love others.

STEP INTO HIS RHYTHM

"Seek first the kingdom of God and His righteousness, and all these things shall be added to you."
MATTHEW 6:33 NKJV

Have you ever been a substitute teacher? You come into a classroom that you don't know, with lesson plans penned from a foreign brain, and systems and flows that are completely unknown. It can be intimidating. We don't need to experience this in our Christian lives because we are familiar with how God works. Pause for a moment and reflect over the ways God has moved and worked in your life before. Look to the teacher and remember the flow of the classroom of your life, or think back over your experiences and see the lesson plans he wrote for you.

Now, take the biggest concern that you have right now: finances, deadlines, or personal relationships. By stepping in and trying to take charge, you are like a substitute teacher trying to understand why Jimmy must sit in the front, or why Mrs. Smith decided to take a particular direction with History. You are forcing your mold into a mold that doesn't fit! In your Christian walk, step in rhythm with the kingdom of God. Realize that he has things under control. Allow your plans to be surrendered to him and experience a life that is blessed through doing it his way.

Jesus, I am committed to walking in rhythm with your beat. Thank you that I can confidently give you control of my current situation.

STORIES OF HOPE

Worship Christ as Lord of your life. And if someone asks about your Christian hope, always be ready to explain it.
1 PETER 3:15 NLT

When good things happen to us, we share the news! We know who is having a baby, which football team won, or who got the promotion. We hear of people who have conquered sickness or found a new house. Too often, we don't communicate this news as being really good! When sickness leaves, we simply say we are better. When the promotion comes, we say a quick thanks and move on. What if we examined our lives and recognized the good news as God moving and creating opportunities for hope? You didn't just get better; God restored your health and was there for you while it was hard.

When we see discipleship and evangelism as huge tasks for great people, we miss out on the everyday opportunities to share good news. Jot down some ways the Lord has been faithful to you. When these stories come up with co-workers, students, or friends, tell the real story. The story of hope is backed by the power of the Holy Spirit and is able to change lives. Let the small stories be a banner waved of the greater hope within you—Jesus Christ.

Thank you, Lord, for being involved in my everyday life! I want to give you praise daily for your work and your power within me.

BY YOUR SIDE

In my trouble I cried to the LORD,
and he answered me.
PSALM 120:1 NASB

"I've given seventeen years, God, how much more do you want?" an exasperated special education teacher declared. "I had a rough Monday, but he brought a great Friday, reminding me of my love for these boys. But it took a long time with God and a few tears to get there." No matter how long you've been teaching or what kind of children you have in your care, breaking points come. A job of pouring out means that sometimes you are empty, and in those times you may need to shed some tears, free and open before the Lord.

In ancient Hebrew culture, it was common for friends to sit together in silence during times of grief. Sometimes the answer may be silent tears or a waterfall of emotions. Never let shame keep you from expressing those feelings. Find a place you can go—your closet, a bathroom, a walk through the woods or down the street—and let out your frustrations to the Lord, just like you would to a good friend over a cup of coffee. Then let the silence sit next to you, knowing that he will either speak or grieve with you, but be ever confident that he is near.

Jesus, thank you that you are near and that you never leave, even if you are silent. Sit by my side and remind me of your presence in my time of trouble.

ANCHORED BY CHRIST

"I have told you all this so that you may have peace in me. Here on earth you will have many trials and sorrows. But take heart, because I have overcome the world."

JOHN 16:33 NLT

Have you ever been grieving or upset when someone offers that token word that everything will be ok? There is something inside that rebels when we hear that because deep down we fear that everything may not be ok. Life is not full of guarantees. It might be blatantly obvious, like the loss of a loved one, or it may be the hidden ambiguity of strained relationships. Either way, we don't find comfort in clichés.

We desire peace and try to glean it from knowing why our situation is happening. The craving for knowledge rises when the aroma of the world's trouble assaults us. When that craving comes, find out where your strength is anchored. Do you search desperately for the answer to the situation? Do you numb the pain with food, social media, shopping, or work? True peace is trusting in the one who controls all things. Can you rest in the knowledge that Christ is in control? In your time of trouble, listen past the well-intentioned phrases and be anchored by the words of Christ.

Speak your truth to me, Jesus. I acknowledge that you are in control of my situation, and I anchor myself in you.

FACING THE STORM TOGETHER

Let us not neglect our meeting together, as some people do, but encourage one another, especially now that the day of his return is drawing near.

HEBREWS 10:25 NLT

Those who have grown up in hurricane-prone areas have learned that when warnings come, they need to board up windows, secure their belongings, and hunker down in safety to wait out the fierce storm. In these times, the comfort of others can make a darkened room cozy, or even pleasant.

When you look at the news for ten minutes or less, you can sense the warning of spiritual hurricanes. It says in the Bible that the last days are not going to be easy. People will be selfish, cynical, crude, and violent. Instead of hunkering down alone, venture out, light a candle, and gather others around. In a church family, you will find spiritual mothers with candles, spiritual fathers ready to worship, and brothers and sisters in the faith ready to play the game of life with you. You will even find little siblings needing protection and reassurance in their own storms of life. Why stay alone in the storm when you don't have to?

The world is dark around me, God. Thank you that you have given me a spiritual family to be near to. Help me to be vulnerable and loving toward them as we grow together in true fellowship.

UPROOT RESENTMENT

Those with good sense are slow to anger,
and it is their glory to overlook an offense.

PROVERBS 19:11 NRSV

Rumors are an unfortunate product of any workplace with more than two employees. Gossip, misunderstandings, and disagreements can become a wildfire of damaging words. When these arrows are aimed at you, there is a choice to make. It is easy to take offense, but if you allow that root to burrow in your heart, it can choke out your joy and peace. You can replay those words over and over until they consume you, or you can hit the delete button and focus on having grace for others. It isn't easy to be objective when you are hurt, but the ability to recognize that people make mistakes can go a long way toward experiencing healing.

If you feel that bitterness has taken root in your heart, try memorizing this verse or ones like it. Remember that the Holy Spirit is there to enable you to be gracious. Overlooking others' mistakes can bring transformation to your thought life, freeing up energy that dwells on the offense to be used instead for the glory of God! Pray today for roots of resentment to be found and for the strength to uproot them.

Holy Spirit, help me to overlook the wrongs done against me. Let your love and peace bloom as I reflect your grace toward others.

UNLEASH YOUR GIFTS

Having then gifts differing according to the grace that is given to us, let us use them.

ROMANS 12:6 NKJV

We all love to see children come alive. This is probably one of the reasons you chose to teach in the first place. Watching a child discover a passion is a beautiful thing. Joy bubbles out of them and overflows into those around them. Praying for these kinds of moments for our students and children is wonderful, but don't neglect to pray the same for yourself. Hidden beneath the façade of the familiar are your gifts. The things that catch your eye, things that come easy, things that seem as ordinary as breathing to you could be strengths lying dormant.

God rejoices over your expressed gifts like we do over children's finger paintings. Don't hold your gifts up to the measuring stick of this world; hold them up to your heavenly Father. He delights in seeing you fully alive and it gives him glory for you to be living in fulfillment. Is there a gift that you have been neglecting lately? Pinpoint it and give it special time this week. Thank God for creating you with many gifts and ask him to create opportunities for you to use them.

Thank you, Creator God, that you have given me many gifts! Help me to know what they are and to use them for the glory of your kingdom.

SOURCE OF COURAGE

Whenever I am afraid, I will trust in You.
In God (I will praise His word),
In God I have put my trust;
I will not fear.
PSALM 56:3-4 NKJV

A good history book will often have a timeline that documents many important historical figures and events that have occurred from as far back as can be recorded. Many of these prominent people and events are centered on a simple word: war. History is woven with many stories of soldiers who stood up for their cause and medals of courage to prove it. At home, women courageously put themselves to work to support their families and towns. These stories can inspire us toward bravery.

The Old Testament also tells stories of bravery and strength. Joshua led the nation of Israel into the Promised Land, David defeated the entire Philistine army with a single stone, and Ruth left her homeland behind to enter into the unknown. In these stories, we find a similar theme: people of courage put their trust in a faithful God. Do you need to be brave today? Jesus is your source. When you are facing overwhelming situations, hand your fear over to Jesus and let him strengthen you to step out in courage.

Jesus, let me be brave today by casting aside fear, holding on to your hands, and stepping out of the boat. Help me to keep my eyes focused on you.

EYES ON THE PRIZE

I have fought the good fight, I have finished the course, I have kept the faith; in the future there is laid up for me the crown of righteousness, which the Lord, the righteous Judge, will award to me on that day; and not only to me, but also to all who have loved His appearing.

2 TIMOTHY 4:7 NASB

We know that the Olympic Games originated from the center of Greece. Similar to the Olympic Games were the Isthmian games, held biannually in Corinth, a place where the apostle Paul spent a lot of his time. Paul would have seen the athletic training, work, and preparation that went into this event. Paul compares life to the games that surrounded him. He illustrates the spiritual race that has a strong focus on the finish line.

How is your great endurance race going? Are you trying to do too much, too fast? Are you properly fueling up for the run? Are you injured, frustrated, or distracted? It helps to keep your mind on the goal, and that is the prize of eternity. Take some time to examine endurance runners. Find the parallels between those runners and Paul's life in Christ. Be encouraged to keep your eyes on the true prize: a crown of righteousness and eternal life with Jesus Christ.

Keep my eyes on the true prize, Lord. Free me from the frustrations and distractions that keep me from enduring this race. Help me to live with the confidence that I will one day say I have fought the good fight and kept the faith.

THE MORNING LIGHT

Whatever is true, whatever is noble, whatever is right, whatever is pure, whatever is lovely, whatever is admirable—if anything is excellent or praiseworthy—think about such things.

PHILIPPIANS 4:8 NIV

The book of Psalms gives us a good sense of the varying emotional states of King David. We see many moments of despair that seem to come from shame, fear, and confusion. We also read, however, that most of these darker moments end in hope. When David describes his soul as downcast, he sets his sight on the goodness of God. The promises of God are what get him through until the morning.

The promises of God are excellent, noble, lovely and true: eternal life, comfort, strength and peace. Search out Scripture for his promises and keep them at the forefront of your mind. Trust in God's mercy; rejoice in his salvation; live in his love. Dwell on the goodness of God each day so that in moments of darkness, the promise of the morning light will shine through.

Jesus, bring your Word continually to my mind. Help me to focus my thoughts on your promises that are right and true.

TAKE THAT LEAP

Faith is confidence in what we hope for and assurance about what we do not see.
HEBREWS 11:1 NIV

We all have hopes, dreams, and plans for our lives. Many of us feel as though the dreams have been buried. Some dreams may be on hold because the timing is not right yet. You may have bigger hopes, such as a family member's salvation or a better career, or smaller hopes like surviving a rough patch or being able to take a break.

Hope is a great motivator, but we need to be able to move to faith. Faith is the tangible outworking of our hope. It is that first step. It's the little kid jumping into a mud puddle, knowing his boots will keep him warm. Faith is saying yes to things that move us forward and letting go of the fear or circumstance that hold us back. Sometimes faith can be waiting patiently for the right timing. When that time comes, put your hope into action! God wants to move and work in your life, and he wants to fulfil the dreams that have come from him. Take the leap, land in the puddle, and you will find yourself dancing in the rain.

Jesus, I pray for strength and boldness to take steps toward the hopes and dreams that you have placed within me. Fill me with faith and assurance of a wonderful future.

MARCH

We boast in the hope
of the glory of God.
And hope does not
put us to shame.

Romans 5:2, 5 NIV

FREED THROUGH FORGIVENESS

"Whenever you stand praying, forgive,
if you have anything against anyone, so that
your Father also who is in heaven may forgive you."
MARK 11:25 ESV

When you drop a piece of fruit on the ground, you can easily bruise it. If you don't cut out the bruise, it will begin to affect the rest of the fruit. If you place it back in the fruit bowl, it will quickly begin to spoil the other fruit. Damage needs to be dealt with swiftly.

Studies have shown that a variety of physical illnesses and emotional ills can be traced back to grudges and resentment that we continue to hold on to. Hurts, even as far back as our childhoods, can greatly affect the choices we make in our adult lives. We must forgive others if we want release from the pain. The result is freedom.

Lord, I ask for help with resentment. Help me to forgive the past and the people who have wronged me. Fill my heart with freedom and peace. Let me look to the future with joy.

CONFESSIONS

You, Lord, are good, and ready to forgive,
and abundant in mercy to all those who call upon You.

PSALM 86:5 NKJV

We have many different levels of punishment for wrongdoing at school. Moving to a different desk, standing outside the classroom, being sent to the principal's office, detention, and worse yet, suspension. While we know these punishments act as disincentives for bad behavior, they also offer a way to forgiveness. It gives the child a chance to say sorry and move toward reconciliation.

Guilt can be debilitating. When we have unconfessed sin in our lives, it eats away at us. The shame we feel can be overwhelming. God is standing ready to forgive everything we have done. He isn't counting up mistakes and keeping a tally, but he patiently waits for us to come to him. Unburden yourself of sin. God's mercy and compassion are unconditional.

Heavenly Father, there are so many times I need forgiveness. I am calling on you for mercy. Thank you for standing ready to forgive me of all the wrong I have done. Thank you for lifting the heavy burden of guilt and shame and allowing me to start afresh.

THE JOY OF GIVING

It is more blessed to give than to receive.
ACTS 20:35 NIV

This verse is often cited when talking about tithing—giving back to God a portion of our earnings. It's good practice and a wise idea. But Paul wasn't only talking about money. He was talking about giving your time, skills, and abilities to help the disadvantaged, the poor, and one another. Paul reminds us that we are blessed when we give of ourselves.

You have been given special talents through your education and experience that you can share with others. It may involve hard work, but the reward will be mighty. You will be blessed.

Lord Jesus, help me to see to the needs of those around me. I want to be able to help. Thank you for giving me talents that make me unique. Help me find ways to bless others.

A GENTLE RESPONSE

A gentle answer turns away wrath,
but a harsh word stirs up anger.
PROVERBS 15:1 NIV

Nothing can rile up a student more quickly than harsh words or a severe scolding. They become sullen, stop listening, and may respond in anger themselves. If we're honest, many times we tend to react the same way. God's wisdom tells us to use gentleness and kindness when we deal with others. Peace and compassion can assist us more in our daily relationships than irritation and annoyance.

Gentleness requires self-discipline. We have to put it into practice on a daily basis. You will have many opportunities to practice a gentle response if you are teaching a class or a number of classes in one day! Rely on the Holy Spirit for grace in these situations and be encouraged that he is always gentle with you.

Lord, help me keep a gentle spirit. Let my words be encouraging and cheerful. I want my classroom to be calm place. Help me to pause a moment before I react in unkindness, so I can make my classroom an oasis of peace.

THANKFULNESS IN EVERYTHING

Everything God created is good, and nothing is to be rejected if it is received with thanksgiving.
1 TIMOTHY 4:4 NIV

Anne Frank and her family hid from the Nazis in a tiny attic for more than two years. During that time, she had only a small window from which to view the outside world. In her diary, she speaks of the wonder of seeing a bird flying through the sky, of a tiny flower spied across the street. She writes that even in her circumstances she found good in people. In that frightening place, she found a thankful heart. She saw the world around her as a place of amazement.

In the midst of turmoil, there is always something to be grateful for. God wants us to see the good around us and have a thankful heart. What can you view from your small window today? Is it a wonder of nature, the help of a friend, or the eagerness of a child? Allow yourself to see the good of God's creation and enter today with a grateful heart.

Dear Lord, thank you for creating me. Let me see the goodness all around me. Give me a heart of thanksgiving for the many blessings in my life.

COLLECTIVE WISDOM

Let the wise listen and add to their learning,
and let the discerning get guidance.

PROVERBS 1:5 NIV

Knowledge is not static. We add to the collective wisdom of the world on a daily basis. New discoveries are taking place, methods are being analyzed, and processes are updated. Development happens so quickly these days; it's enough to make your head spin.

An astute person never stops learning. Seek out those who are experts in the field of education, in science and math. Listen to the artists, the writers, and the musicians. Allow yourself to be mentored by a wiser, more experienced person. Ask God to give you discernment for the right people to learn from, so what you absorb is true to his Word.

Dear God, put a thirst for knowledge in me. Help me to find mentors to train me. Let me seek wise counsel from those in my field. Never let me lose my quest for what is true and comes from you. Thank you for teaching me from your Word.

ENCOURAGE GOOD HABITS

Warn those who are idle and disruptive, encourage the disheartened, help the weak, be patient with everyone.

1 THESSALONIANS 5:14 NIV

An important thing for anyone to learn is good study habits. This includes how to listen, how to read and comprehend, and how to apply what we learn. These are lessons that will help us throughout our lives. What an easy task it is to encourage those who are eager to learn!

It can be difficult to watch students who are disruptive or lazy in your class. It can be one of many frustrations of your vocation, but motivating these students to learn and having higher expectations of them is in their best interests. Bad habits tend to get worse as time goes on. Teach your students good habits and watch them thrive.

Lord, help me to have the courage to help my students. Let me encourage those who need more motivation. Thank you for giving me the opportunity to infuse your Word in these lives. Give me wisdom to be a good role model.

SOUL FOOD

Behold, God is my helper;
The LORD is the sustainer of my soul.
PSALM 54:4 NASB

When we are in trouble, God is our helper. He will stand by us and protect us from danger. We can ask him for help when we are perplexed, unsure, or confused. He is more than willing to support us in our endeavors. He can assist us in changing our habits, healing our bodies, and easing our minds.

If we lack wisdom, we can ask God for it. The Bible tells us that he will meet all of our needs. Best of all, he will nourish and sustain our very souls.

God, I need your help. Sometimes I need advice and direction. When I am confused, I welcome your help. Thank you for watching over me and knowing my needs even before I see them. Please keep my soul safe in you.

HUMBLE HOSPITALITY

When God's people are in need, be ready to help. Always be eager to practice hospitality.

ROMANS 12:13 NLT

It can become a point of anxiety to share your home. When you compare your house with pictures on Pinterest, or your cooking to Martha Stewart's, you can be left feeling inadequate. Here's a little known secret... it doesn't matter one bit. The Bible doesn't just suggest we practice hospitality; we are exhorted to do so. A house doesn't have to be spotless and a meal doesn't have to be fancy.

Sharing what you have with those in need benefits them, but it also blesses you. If you have an extra bed, you can make it available to someone passing through or to a friend when it's too late to drive home. It may be giving soup and bread to a new mother or someone who is ill. God is interested in your willingness to be kind and helpful to those around you. Look for ways you can practice hospitality.

Dear Lord, I want to be available to offer hospitality to those in need. Help me to find ways I can help others. Give me wisdom to discern the needs of those people around me. Thank you for providing for me.

AN HONEST REPUTATION

I always try to do what I believe is right before God and people.
ACTS 24:16 NCV

When we familiarize ourselves with Scripture, what is right or wrong is more easily discerned. As children of God, we wish to do what is right in his eyes. Jesus tells us that the two greatest commandments are to love God with all of our hearts and to love others as we love ourselves.

Putting the Lord first in our lives—loving him and serving him—should be our first priority. Then our dealings with those we meet will be in their best interests. We can earn respect and admiration with our honesty.

God, thank you for first loving me. Help me to treat others honestly and with respect. I want my reputation to reflect your righteousness.

WHITE LIES

The king is pleased with words from righteous lips;
he loves those who speak honestly.
PROVERBS 16:13 NLT

It's easy to tell a white lie, especially if it does no apparent harm. Perhaps you are trying to spare someone's feelings. Telling one "little" lie can lead to another, and then another, and the downward spiral begins.

How much easier it is to purpose to always, *always* tell the truth. God loves honesty and those who speak the truth. The truth need not be harsh or brutal, but through gentleness and sincerity, it will have great power.

Oh God, help me to be truthful at all times. I want my devotion to you to be apparent in my words. May my honesty reflect your character and may you find pleasure in my speech.

RIGHTEOUS RESPECT

We want to live honorably in everything we do.
HEBREWS 13:18 NLT

Living honorably is one sure way to garner respect. We admire those whose word can be trusted, whose reputation is blameless. As a teacher, we become role models to our students and others around us. There are eyes on us every day. Will they want to emulate our behavior, respect and admire us? Or will they wonder about our core beliefs?

What godly characteristics do we exhibit? Are we truthful, helpful, sincere, and friendly? Do we share with others? Are we satisfied and thankful for what we have? A good reputation is a treasure that brings honor to the Lord.

Oh Lord, you are worthy of our praise. Help me to know your Word and to use it as a guide in my life. I want to live honorably. I want a good reputation. Please help me to make right choices.

OVERFLOW

May the God of hope fill you with all joy and peace as you trust in him, so that you may overflow with hope by the power of the Holy Spirit.

ROMANS 15:13 NIV

Hope is more than yearning for truth; it is an expectation that God's Word is a certainty that can be counted upon. The reality of God's grace and peace is a fact that should fill us with joy!

When we put our trust in God, doubts and uncertainty should be pushed aside as the Holy Spirit fills us with hope. If distrust creeps in, be reminded of God's mighty love for you and the promise of eternal life with him.

Lord, thank you for the knowledge of your love and protection from doubts. Help me to remember how much you love me and to know the certainty of your grace and joy.

HEROES

"Let your light shine before others, so that they may see your good works and give glory to your Father who is in heaven."
MATTHEW 5:14-16 ESV

Who are your heroes? Who inspires you? For many young people, heroes are celebrities or sports figures who have a superstar image. When you live a godly life, those around you notice.

The students in your charge are looking to you as an example. Let your life be an inspiration to them. They need better role models than what media supplies. Show them the love of God through your actions and deeds.

God, remind me that I have many eyes on me. Help me keep my actions worthy of being your child. Thank you for showing me in your Word how I should act and what to do. Please give me the enabling power to be a shining light for your glory.

FULFILLED FOLLOWERS

The righteous walk in integrity—
happy are the children who follow them!
PROVERBS 20:7 NRSV

Teachers are more than experts in their field of study. They are counselors and role models to their students. When they are upright, honorable, caring, and kindhearted, they create a classroom even more conducive to learning. Students are eager to come to class, and are happy and excited to learn.

Show your class, by example, that you are genuine and sincere, and they will be happy following your lead.

O Lord, I want my children to see you in my life. Help me to be honorable and to walk in integrity. Thank you for the opportunity to affect the lives of the students entrusted to me. May they be happy and eager to learn what I have to teach them.

TRUST THE WAIT

Let integrity and uprightness preserve me,
For I wait for You.
PSALM 25:21 NKJV

In our walk with the Lord, we depend on him to help us through times of trouble, confusion, or fear. We rely on God to meet our daily needs. We trust him to keep his promises to us. Sometimes we call out to him to help us and we fear he fails us. We seek immediate answers and instant results. We wait on God impatiently.

When it seems that God has not heard you, it is time to stand still. Listen and wait. The Lord *has* heard and knows exactly what you require. Your job is to take a godly stance and continue in the path he has set for you. He will make the answer known in due time. Your patience and assurance will be rewarded.

Dear God, sometimes I am impatient with you. I need to trust that you hear me when I pray, and you have my best interests deeply held in your loving heart. Please let me be comforted in your Word as I wait to hear your voice.

RANDOM ACTS OF KINDNESS

Be kind and compassionate to one another.
EPHESIANS 4:32 NIV

When we belong to the Lord, we mirror the qualities of the Holy Spirit. Kindness is among those listed. Being kind to others is a direct result of the love of God in our lives.

Ask yourself if you are thoughtful, considerate, and kind. Try to find little ways to bless others. The recipient will appreciate any small deed, thoughtfully executed. A random act of kindness is offering an unexpected gift or performing a compassionate act, often to a stranger. Be deliberate in your actions and look for opportunities to offer kindness.

Dear God, thank you for your many kindnesses to me. Help me to find ways to be thoughtful in my words and my actions. I want to bless others in helpful ways. Help me to find opportunities to show compassion.

BESIEGED BY KINDNESS

Blessed be the LORD,
For He has shown me His marvelous kindness
in a strong city!

PSALM 31:21 NKJV

Have you ever felt trapped? A time when there is danger on the right and wickedness on the left, peril before and behind? You may not be in a city besieged by a hostile army, but sometimes it can feel as if you are in the midst of a war with evil.

God will meet you where you are with lovingkindness. He will show you compassion and gentleness, drawing you into his arms of safety. When you feel afraid, you can draw near to him in prayer. You can tell him your fears, secure in the knowledge that he only wants the best for you.

Lord, thank you for caring for me. Thank you that I can depend on you to show me kindness and love. In times of trouble, I want to depend on you.

THE BEST INSPIRATIONAL BOOK

*He gives wisdom to the wise and knowledge
to the discerning.*
DANIEL 2:21 NIV

Wisdom is available to each of us if we spend our time studying the Scriptures. In the Bible, we find how to treat others and what to do if we are poorly regarded. In its pages, we find sound health advice, financial help, and counsel for teachers, bosses, and parents. We can discover the truth of healthy relationships, and be inspired and encouraged in how to deal with sadness and fears.

Some may say that the Bible is a fairy tale or a book for long ago, but a wise follower of Jesus knows that it is a truly inspired book of wisdom and knowledge. Blessings will accompany the understanding that is found within it.

God, I want to discern your wisdom for my life. Help me to regularly search and study the Scriptures to know more. Help me to learn from you. Guide me in my studies.

PREPARE FOR GROWTH

Be joyful. Grow to maturity. Encourage each other.
Live in harmony and peace. Then the God of love
and peace will be with you.

2 CORINTHIANS 13:11 NLT

In the spring, gardeners prepare the soil with a great deal of hope and expectation. They plant the seeds, cover them with dirt, and apply fertilizer and water. They are overjoyed when the first baby sprouts of green emerge from the ground. They pamper those sprouts by shielding them from direct sun, protecting them from the birds and continuing to provide water and plant food. The gardener gathers with other horticulturists and they share their experiences. In a few short months, the garden is resplendent with flowers and vegetables. The colors are gorgeous and the produce is luscious.

This analogy is a lot like your teaching environment. As you prepare, be expectant of growth. As you teach, encourage and nourish your students. As you approach hardship, seek out the advice of experienced teachers. Be thankful as you see the beautiful development and allow the God of peace to revive you with his love.

Lord, help me to see my classroom more like that garden, gorgeous and full of good taste. Grant me your love and peace as I continue to encourage growth in the lives of these students.

CREDENTIALS

Those who get wisdom do themselves a favor,
and those who love learning will succeed.
PROVERBS 19:8 NCV

As teachers, it is our job to impart learning to our students. We trained to obtain college degrees and certificates that state we are credentialed to teach. Do we then proceed in a long career, completely satisfied with our methods and practices? Of course not!

Graduation, certification, and your first classroom is just the very beginning of a lifelong quest for learning more about your field, teaching techniques, and professional knowledge. In order to be a successful instructor you should never stop acquiring knowledge. A thirst for learning will lead to greater success—this promise is in God's word!

Dear Lord, thank you for making me a teacher. Keep my brain functioning so that I may fill it with knowledge. I don't ever want to think I know it all; I want to be humble and seek wisdom. Teach me your ways, O God.

SUPREME QUALITIES

*Three things will last forever—faith, hope, and love—and
the greatest of these is love.*
1 CORINTHIANS 13:13 NLT

The Bible says that three things will last forever: our faith in
God, our hope in eternal life, and love. It also reminds us that
the utmost quality is love. Love has many facets. Adoration,
worship, care, devotion, mercy, and grace are but a few. God's
love for us is everlasting. He has loved us from before the
beginning and will continue loving us throughout eternity.

Jesus told us that out of all of the commandments, two
are the greatest. The first is to love God with our entire being
and the other is to love others as we love ourselves. Without
the Father's love we would be lost, with no hope of salvation.
Faith, hope, and love will last forever, but love is the greatest!

**Lord God, thank you for the great love you show me daily.
Help me to love others. Show me how to share your love
with the people I meet. Thank you for making a way for me
to live with you forever.**

BOUNDLESS LOVE

May the Lord make your love for one another and for all people grow and overflow.
1 THESSALONIANS 3:12 NLT

When we open our heart to others, we make ourselves vulnerable. We can be hurt or embarrassed. You may be shy, insecure, or guarded and this can make it difficult to open up. The Lord can handle your limitations because there is no limit on his love for you. His love is boundless.

When you feel inadequate to love others, ask the Lord for help. He delights in helping his children. The simple act of showing kindness can fill our own hearts to overflowing.

God, I want to show your love to others. Provide me with opportunities to do so today. Thank you for showing me your love. Help me to share that love with those around me.

STEADFAST LOVE

You, O Lord, are good and forgiving,
abounding in steadfast love to all who call upon you.
PSALM 86:5 ESV

God's love is different than our definition of love. His love is unconditional. He loves us before we love him; he loves us while we are still wallowing in sin. The world's definition of love is based on feelings, attraction, and whim. This kind of love is fickle and often changes the object of its affection.

God loves us always and forever. His mercy is unwavering, resolute, and persistent. We can count on it. It is a good thing that the Lord's love is abiding and steadfast. He forgives us and then forgives us again. God's mercy and grace are available when we call upon him. If you need to seek forgiveness, just ask the Lord. He abounds in love.

God, sometimes I fail and I need to ask forgiveness. Thank you for your abundant love for me. Thank you that I can count on your mercy daily.

LEARN FROM THE MENTOR

I will instruct you and teach you in the way you should go;
I will counsel you with my loving eye on you.

PSALM 32:8 NIV

As you trained to be a teacher, you probably had some mentors. There may have been counselors who took an interest in you and helped you along the way. They would have offered wisdom and helped you become a better instructor. Perhaps you are now mentoring young people in their life journey.

God wants to be your mentor. He wants to help you each day, and he has your best interests at heart. The Lord can lead you in any situation because he can see down the path and ahead to the future.

God, thank you for keeping your loving eye on me. Help me to ask you for help and wisdom during the day. I want to mature in your ways.

RELAX AND BREATHE!

Rest in the LORD and wait patiently for Him…
Those who wait for the LORD, they will inherit the land.
PSALM 37:7-9 NASB

We live in a world that provides instant gratification. Fast food, quick Internet, and all kinds of shopping is at our fingertips. We can be instantly supplied with what we want. In this whirlwind world, we need rest and refreshment. Take a minute to breathe. Listen to the birds, and look at the beauty of the flowers. Attune yourself to God. He wants to give you sweet relaxation to calm your spirit and feed your soul.

The rat race is a never-ending revolving wheel of busyness that does us more harm than good. Seek the refreshment of the Lord in his Word. Patiently listen for him to speak to you. He will instruct you. Slow down and open your heart. God is waiting to give you all you yearn for.

O Lord, help me to slow down and listen to you. When I want instant answers, help me to be patient. Let me learn to wait. Thank you for refreshing my soul.

STILLNESS OF HEART

The LORD gives strength to his people;
the LORD blesses his people with peace.
PSALM 29:11 NIV

Teaching days can be hectic. We may be bombarded by demanding students at an inopportune moment, just as a note is received from the office about a form that is needed *now*. A girl gets a bloody nose. You can't find the book you need. But you have trained for this, you know what to do and how to stand in the center of the chaos, serene and tranquil.

Just as God has helped equip you to face the challenges of your day, he can help you to find the peace and harmony you need. When tough times come, seek that quiet place in the stillness of your heart and calm yourself. God wants to bless you with peace. He knows your soul yearns for calm and quiet. Remember that this place of serenity is where he can best minister to you.

God, thank you for equipping me with strength and knowledge to do my job. Help me to find a place of serenity and calm when circumstances get hectic. Grant me patience and peace to quiet my heart and deal with my surroundings.

EXPLORE HIS PROMISES

The hope of eternal life, which God, who does not lie,
promised before the beginning of time.
TITUS 1:2 NIV

According to one person's count, God has made over 3500 promises in the Bible. That's a lot of promises. Some have to do with finances, health, overcoming problems, training children and more. But the most important promise that God makes is the one in which he has promised us eternal life.

God has given us his assurance that when we belong to him we will spend eternity with him. He wanted us to know that we could take him at his word, so he sacrificed his Son. What a sign of God's great love for each of us! Take some time today to explore the Bible for a few of the promises of God. Allow yourself to trust in a God who keeps his word.

Father God, thank you for loving me so much that you gave your Son to reveal to me the promise of eternal life! Help me to discover your promises and to trust in your Word.

RESPECT YOUR SUPERIORS

Appreciate those who diligently labor among you, and have charge over you in the Lord and give you instruction... esteem them very highly in love because of their work. Live in peace with one another.

1 THESSALONIANS 5:12-13

Each day, there are superiors working behind the scenes to make jobs easier. They perform a variety of rolls that enhance working conditions and physical infrastructure. They manage the record keeping and supplies needed to function in the classroom. We need to value them and remember that the work they do eases our load. They are our partners in education.

The Bible reminds us that we need to show our superiors respect and pray for them, as their responsibilities can be difficult and complex. You can also help create a better working environment for everyone by modeling a peacemaker's mentality. Rather than complaining, be encouraging and help to keep the peace. Rely on God's strength to treat others the way you would like to be treated.

Dear Lord, help me to show respect for those in positions over me. They work hard to help me do my job well. Remind me of their assistance. Thank you for the help you give me each day.

CORPORATE COOPERATION

*Have confidence in your leaders and submit to their
authority, because they keep watch over you as those who
must give an account. Do this so that their work will be a
joy, not a burden, for that would be of no benefit to you.*

HEBREWS 13:17 NIV

Forms, tests, requests, reports. These are just a few of
those extra things that a teacher is required to do that seem
to take away from quality teaching time. Admittedly, it is
easy to let these tasks slide. Have you realized, however, that
performing these jobs well and on time shows respect to
those in authority above you? They also have a job to do that
depends on your cooperation.

God has charged you to perform your duties to the best
of your abilities. When you carry these out in a timely manner
and allow your superiors to do their jobs well, God is pleased.
Try to be a joy to those around you in everything you do.

**Lord God, thank you for my job. Renew my love of
teaching and everything that goes with this responsibility.
Thank you for my superiors and hard work. Help me to
support and respect them. I want to be a joy to them and
not a burden.**

TONGUE-TIED

We all make many mistakes. For if we could control our tongues, we would be perfect and could also control ourselves in every other way.

JAMES 3:2 NLT

Oh, that little tongue of ours! It gets us into the biggest trouble. We use our tongue to tell little white lies, gossip, argue, and speak before thinking. These are all reasons for us to pause and use a little self-control. We need to use our head and our heart to bring our tongues into obedience. We need to learn to pause so we encourage instead of chastise.

How often do we speak and later wish we could take back what we said? The lack of self-control shows a need to develop our character and grow in God's way. A sure way to help us do the right thing is to read his Word. Psalms and Proverbs are full of wisdom and understanding. Experience how these simple yet profound words can help you in your daily life.

God, help me to learn more self-control. Keep my tongue honest and pure. I want to be a blessing to those around me.

APRIL

Let all those rejoice

who put their trust in You;

Let them ever shout for joy,

because You defend them;

Let those also who love Your name

Be joyful in You.

PSALM 5:11 NKJV

YOU ARE APPRECIATED

> *God is not unjust so as to overlook your work and the love*
> *that you have shown for his name in serving the saints,*
> *as you still do.*
> HEBREWS 6:10 ESV

A teacher's job is that of a helper. You help students gain wisdom, obtain knowledge, and acquire skills to last them a lifetime. You put in countless hours and extra time on weekends and even vacation time. Sometimes it seems like a thankless job. You might feel unappreciated.

The Lord watches and knows the hard work you put in. He sees your service and remembers you always. He sees your heart and knows the love you have for your students. Be blessed, knowing that your heavenly Father is pleased with you.

O God, help me not to be discouraged when I feel unappreciated. Remind me of your love for me. I want to teach my students well. Give me wisdom to do a good job.

CONTINUAL CONTACT WITH JESUS

Rejoice always, pray without ceasing, in everything give thanks; for this is the will of God in Christ Jesus for you.

1 THESSALONIANS 5:16-18 NKJV

Look. Cover. Write. Check. This is a simple strategy that some elementary teachers use to help children learn their spelling. The words give the children a way of learning how to develop their skills and grow in their understanding. In the same way, the apostle Paul gives us a few words to help us in our walk. Rejoice. Pray. Give thanks. This list of instructions is for our benefit. We are reminded to do these things always, without ceasing, and in every situation. It might sound impossible, but we start by putting it into practice.

The key to being happy, satisfied, and grateful is to remain in contact with God. Our heart and soul belong to Jesus. We achieve depth in relationship through rejoicing, praying, and giving thanks. A fulfilled life is one that is continually in the will of God.

Dear Lord, thank you for loving me. I want to walk in your will all my life. Remind me to rejoice and be in constant prayer. May I be truly thankful for everything that comes my way.

SAFE IN HIM

The LORD is for me; he will help me.
It is better to take refuge in the LORD
than to trust in people.

PSALM 118:7-8 NLT

There is a new scam every minute. Mail fraud, internet con, and theft are frequently on the news. People let you down. It is difficult to have confidence in others because we may be disappointed.

We need to put our ultimate faith in the Lord. When someone misses a deadline, we can trust God to have our backs. He can help us in any situation. The Lord will never break a confidence. He is a safe place to unburden our thoughts. We can trust him with our finances and our career questions. God cherishes our hopes and dreams, and offers wise counsel. Take refuge in his care for you.

Lord, when I have questions, let me take refuge in you. Guide me, counsel me, and give me advice. Thank you that my innermost thoughts and dreams are safe with you. I want to trust you more each day.

ULTIMATE TRUTH

Listen, for I will speak of excellent things,
and from the opening of my lips will come right things;
for my mouth will speak truth.

PROVERBS 8:6-7 NKJV

Where does ultimate truth come from? Everywhere we turn someone is using a "fact" to make their point or prove their theory. Many times the same statistics can be used to legitimize both sides of a position; it just depends on how you interpret the numbers. Politicians bend the truth to put forth their own cause. It can be very confusing.

Where do you turn for answers? Who is an authority you can trust? The Bible says that God speaks the truth. We can rely on it. We can depend on our hope of salvation because God has said it. He grants us mercy and grace. He is our deliverer in an evil world. The Lord shows us his lovingkindness by giving us the wisdom and knowledge found in his Word.

God, thank you for giving us the Bible. Help me never to doubt your truth but to search your Word for my answers. Let me test and weigh the truth I hear from the world against your truth.

COMPREHEND THE TRUTH

*Do not be unwise, but understand
what the will of the Lord is.*

EPHESIANS 5:17 NKJV

You may know someone who had a remarkable education with degrees and honors, but somehow they seem to lack common sense. Without a good social understanding, they have problems navigating the everyday world because they can't hold a normal conversation, pay attention as they walk, or dress with any semblance of fashion. They may have much knowledge, but they lack the understanding they need for polite society.

The same is true when we read God's Word. We must not only read it, but also understand what the Lord wants us to learn. Memorizing Scripture is a good idea, but it is also important to comprehend the truth God has for us in a particular verse and commit that to memory as well. Discerning God's will for our lives requires wisdom!

Dear Lord, help me to understand your Word. I want to know your will for my life. Give me a thirst for understanding and a passion for your truth. Thank you for the Scriptures and the treasures to be found in them.

DIG DEEP

Wisdom will enter your heart,
and knowledge will fill you with joy.
PROVERBS 2:10 NLT

A great day in the classroom is when a student's face lights up and says, "*Now* I get it!" They may have known the facts, but just didn't understand until that moment. What joy! This is one of the great rewards of our vocation.

When we read God's Word, we need to ask him for the ability to comprehend what he really wants us to know. Parables are stories told to get a point across. There are lessons for us to learn in Old Testament accounts. We can identify with many of the people of the Bible and the choices they made. Dig deeply into Scripture and you will find treasure there: wisdom, knowledge, and God's will for your life. These bring joy and a closer relationship with the Lord.

God, I want to read more of your Word. Help me to understand the Bible better. Give me wisdom and the knowledge to know you better. Thank you for the joy I have in you.

NOTHING COMPARES

Wisdom is far more valuable than precious jewels.
Nothing else compares with it.
PROVERBS 3:15 TLB

Solomon had a chance to ask God for anything. Instead of riches and glory, he asked for a heart to hear God. God gave him all the wisdom, knowledge, and intellect available. Solomon used this understanding to establish a legal and judicial system unrivaled in his time. He had foreign policy success and a healthy economy at home. He had riches beyond comprehension, but he favored wisdom. He knew that good judgment and understanding was worth more than gold or jewels.

We need to ask God for wisdom. Too often we ask for things. When we gain insight, it is easy to know what is and is not important. With knowledge, priorities reveal themselves, and good judgment allows us freedom from making poor choices.

Lord, sometimes I feel foolish and don't know what to do. Help me seek your wisdom. I want to use good judgment in all that I do. Give me insight to improve my thinking.

STRESS-FREE

*May the Lord of peace himself give you peace
at all times in every way.*

2 Thessalonians 3:16 esv

Worry can fill us with all manner of negative emotions. Anxiety, fear, apprehension, terror, and panic can invade our minds. It can lead to lack of sleep, stomach problems, and even heart ailments. We may dread the very activities that give us pleasure and fulfillment. We long for peace.

If you desire a mind free from worry, you can ask God for peace. He will take your fear and replace it with confidence. He can replace your worries with serenity and harmony in your life. The problems that seem insurmountable will become manageable.

Dear Lord, when worry fills my mind, please give me peace. Thank you for caring for me and helping me at all times and in every way. Let me trust you to fill me with comfort and calm.

APPRECIATING TODAY

"Don't worry about tomorrow, for tomorrow will bring its own worries. Today's trouble is enough for today."
MATTHEW 6:34 NLT

Do you ever wonder "what if?" What if I break my leg? What if my house burns down? What if no one likes me? Thinking about the what ifs can spiral you into a deep, depressive hole.

As children of God, we know that we will spend eternity with him in heaven. He has a special place for each of us, reserved and waiting. We do not need to worry about our future because the Lord already knows what will happen tomorrow and in the days after that. Worry can paralyze us and keep us from appreciating today. Every day has its challenges. By depending on God to hold our fears each day, we can be free from worry about the future.

Dear God, I want freedom from worry. Please rescue me from my fears. I want to depend on you every day. Help me to put my trust in you.

LIGHTEN THE LOAD

Give your burdens to the LORD,
and he will take care of you.
He will not permit the godly to slip and fall.

PSALM 55:22 NLT

Imagine that you are going on walk. You pack a lunch and add a sweater. What about a flashlight in case it gets dark before you return? Maybe you should put in a change of clothing, extra socks, and shoes. You add some more food, a first aid kit, and another bottle of water. By the time you start out you are wearing a backpack and carrying two tote bags. You couldn't possibly have a leisurely or enjoyable walk, weighted down with all those extra things.

We are like that when we pile worry upon worry on our lives. The burden that you carry becomes insurmountable, and you find yourself slipping. The Lord wants to take those worries from you. Give your cares to him. Allow God to handle your worry. He will take care of you. You can count on him.

Lord, sometimes I fill myself with worry. These worries grow until they overwhelm me. Please take my burdens. Lighten my load. Let me trust in you. Thank you for caring for me.

LITTLE ANGELS

"Any of you who welcomes a little child like this because you are Mine, is welcoming Me.... Don't look down upon a single one of these little children. For I tell you that in heaven their angels have constant access to My Father."
MATTHEW 18:5, 10 TLB

Jesus thinks very highly of children and has enlisted angels to take special care of them. That puts a new perspective on things; our teaching environments are filled with angels! Jesus tells us to have pure, trusting hearts, as children do. He admonishes us to keep from taking children lightly or leaving them to stray.

How pleased Jesus is with us as we honor his children and instruct them in life-giving ways. As we honor him and the children he has put in our care, we foster love, respect, and a multitude of other good qualities in the future generation.

Heavenly Father, what an honor it is that you would entrust students to my care. Please give me your heart for them and wisdom and kindness in my instruction of them.

FORWARD-LOOKING

"Go therefore and make disciples of all the nations, baptizing them in the name of the Father and of the Son and of the Holy Spirit, teaching them to observe all things that I have commanded you; and lo, I am with you always."

MATTHEW 28:19-20 NKJV

Have you ever wondered what your students will be doing in twenty years? Some will be in retail. Others will take up trades. Some will become business owners, lawyers, analysts, and technicians. Several will be homemakers, work in the military, invent new items and concepts, and write the news. A handful will be overseas.

The point is this: your faithful dispensation of the Word, and of all that God has given you to share, is important. It will shape nations, and it will come back to you as a blessing. Watch what God does for you. It will exceed, in magnitude and scope, far beyond your imagination and your requests.

Father, you have given me a good reward for my desires: hearts and minds to transform. Please help me glorify you in all I do, so the people in my class glorify you as well. Help them to understand your goodness, and help me to know how to reach them in meaningful ways.

JESUS IS COMING BACK FOR YOU

"I will come back and take you to be with me that you also may be where I am."

JOHN 14:3 NIV

God is gracious in all his ways. He is powerful and kind, and he never breaks his covenant. If Jesus says that he is coming back for you, he really is. And if he says the purpose of him coming back for you is to have you with him, it means he really likes your company and wants to spend forever with you.

There are times we are so glad our day has ended. We close our classroom door, get in the car, and set aside our nightly work long enough to unwind and stop thinking about the day that has just passed. Jesus isn't like that with us. He forgets the bad, cherishes the good, and desires an eternity of more! How good it is to be God's child. He can help us through our days at work, blessing us with every good thing.

God, thank you for loving me so deeply and purely that you want to spend eternity with me. I invite you to make each day your day, and ask you to use me as a vessel to pour out your love to my students, peers, and associates.

JOURNEY OF TRUTH

"If you abide in My word, you are My disciples indeed.
And you shall know the truth,
and the truth shall make you free."
JOHN 8:31-32 NKJV

What a wonderful promise: to know that reading and living out the instruction of the Scriptures will bring us truth that grants us freedom. This is God's truth, not theories. This is spiritual freedom, not physical vacation from burdens or constraints. This is the redemptive life!

When children are born, they know nothing. As they grow, they have to master new thinking and new tasks. They have to think outside of the sphere of their knowledge to get to the next step of understanding. Even Jesus, the only begotten Son of God, underwent a learning process. We have the indescribable joy of co-laboring with Jesus in the role of teacher.

God, thank you for offering me your Word that shows me truth. Help me to be devoted to you and your truth. Help me to carry it forward to my students with grace, humility, and joy.

CALLED TO INTEGRITY

"If you ignore the least commandment and teach others to do the same, you will be called the least in the Kingdom of Heaven. But anyone who obeys God's laws and teaches them will be called great in the Kingdom of Heaven."

MATTHEW 5:19 NLT

Have you ever had to back up your teaching to reiterate a point because you'd forgotten an important fact? Have you stopped a lab to tell students what they needed to accomplish in order to succeed? To backtrack is a natural part of teaching. Teachers aren't perfect, but integrity causes us to retrace our steps and focus the attention of our students to where it should be.

Integrity is important to teaching. This determination to present the truth and fashion an objective, meaningful learning experience is part of God's design within each of us. We inspire and explore, admit weaknesses, and set forth good examples. We do it to create good futures for the people who attend our classes and trust our teaching.

Father, I come to you in Jesus' name. Thank you for embodying integrity, and for creating me to flourish in it. You care for me tenderly; please walk with me through my day and guide me in your integrity.

HIDDEN PLACES

"Nothing is hidden that will not be made manifest, nor is anything secret that will not be known and come to light."
LUKE 8:17 ESV

There are times when it would seem nobody would know if you took a shortcut on a task. Maybe the alternative paperwork is long; maybe just one more signature is needed but not obtainable. God is blessed and pleased with you when you do the right thing and follow the paths of wisdom that lead to peace. Your heavenly Father is glorified in all the good things you do.

Know that if you are doing something in secret, your Lord and Savior will acclaim you in public. For this reason, because of Jesus in your life, you do good things and teach others to do the same. Praise God for his kindness, even in hidden, secret places!

Father, thank you for meeting me in the hidden places in my life. I joyfully submit them to you. Thank you for your honesty toward and through me. May it be infectious within my circles so others can feel safe to embrace honesty and truth as well.

PEACE UPGRADES

"Peace I leave with you; my peace I give you. I do not give to you as the world gives. Do not let your hearts be troubled and do not be afraid."

JOHN 14:27 NIV

Parent-teacher conferences. Performance reviews. Student altercations. Grading disputes. What do these things have in common? They are opportunities for peace upgrades. James 1 says to count it joy when trials occur, because they are springboards to improve your endurance and to perfect you so that your inner person lacks no good thing. As your endurance grows, your peace will temper and grow.

In offering peace, Jesus gave us the right to be optimistic about what he is willing do within us, through us, and for us. We start each day with the attitude that God is for us and that his peace is unshakeable. We step into communion with Jesus early in the day, where his peace resides. As we progress through our responsibilities, we carry that peace within us. We fix our eyes on Jesus, so that we can abide in the safe harbor of connection with him throughout the day.

Jesus, you are so kind and powerful. There is nothing that will happen in my day that will disturb your peace. I choose to enter into that peace with you, Lord. I choose communion with you.

JUST ASK!

"Until now you have not asked for anything in my name.
Ask and you will receive, and your joy will be complete."
JOHN 16:24 NIV

Jesus' followers had been with him for three years.
During this time they learned, walked out his plan, and were
transformed by their relationship with the King of kings. After
so many times of having their needs met by Jesus, these
disciples must have been terribly anxious to think of the days
ahead without him. Although they could not have understood
what Jesus was saying about the Holy Spirit, they did
understand their heavenly Father and that when Jesus prayed,
things happened in truly astonishing ways.

Even today, we know that Jesus, who intercedes for us at all
times, has a name above all names. We have peace in knowing
that God hears our prayers because Jesus carries our hearts
to our heavenly Father. What joy it brings us to know that God
truly loves us and cares to answer our faith-filled prayers!

**Thank you, Jesus, for filling me with your Spirit. I know
I am never alone. You are good and you are kind. Please
help me to make it a wonderful day as I partner with you,
so I can lift up my voice to you in gratitude and praise.**

UNEMBELLISHED

"When he, the Spirit of truth, comes, he will guide you into all the truth."

JOHN 16:13 NIV

The Spirit of God, like Jesus, speaks only what he hears the Father saying. When you feel conviction from doing the wrong thing, and when you feel great peace for doing what is right, it is actually the Holy Spirit telling you what your heavenly Father wants you to know. You can be sure the Holy Spirit is telling you the truth, because he speaks for your wellbeing. He does this strictly by the direction of your heavenly Father, who loves you very dearly.

If people speak for their own cause, it may be assumed that a certain degree of subjectivity colors their speech. When they simply relay the exact message given, we hear data in the rawest transmittable form. This is how the Holy Spirit speaks to us as he lovingly guides us in truth.

God, thank you for living within me in the form of the Holy Spirit. Please help me to be tender toward you, and to understand what you say to me. Make me moldable, and guide me by your gentle hand. Thank you for this wonderful adventure with your Holy Spirit!

DIRTY FEET

"Who is the greater, one who reclines at table or one who serves? Is it not the one who reclines at table? But I am among you as the one who serves."

LUKE 22:27 ESV

As a teacher, you stoop to help children up to the platform of learning. You recite and relearn topics, whether your aim is to adapt to the newest math technique or brush up on your skills so you can process and share information more fluently.

Jesus washed dirty feet and hung out at the tax embezzler's home for the evening. His decision to humbly meet learners where they could receive him was kind and practical. He stayed up late praying for his disciples. He took the role of a servant even though he was the greatest teacher in history.

God, thank you for being a phenomenal example of helpfulness and love. Please speak through my mouth today and work through my hands. Show me your intentions toward my students so I will adopt them as my own.

IMPARTIAL DECISIONS

Be careful to do what is right in the eyes of everyone.
ROMANS 12:17 NIV

Although students love to have favor with teachers, they recognize the importance of your fair, impartial regard. In the end, they know it will render them daily treatment that is equitable, and a year-end grade that stands as a true gauge of their individual progress. It can be hard to give grades, and it can be hard to render decisions.

The Lord rewards your loving integrity and the special care you put into your work. At the end of the day, you will receive a "Well Done!" for being a faithful follower of Christ. God's outcomes are worth today's struggles.

God, thank you for understanding my struggles. Please help me to do what is right in your eyes and to be honorable before people. I know this is a wonderful witnessing tool, and I am glad to be your living epistle.

ON PURPOSE

Be gracious to me, O God,
according to Your lovingkindness;
According to the greatness of Your compassion
blot out my transgressions.

PSALM 51:1 NASB

Everyone stumbles; everyone fails. Rather than glossing over it, Jesus offers us opportunities to be closer to God by responding in honesty and tenderness. Because of God's great mercy, David was able to ask that his transgressions be erased. When David asked God to forgive him, it was because he understood his desperate situation. He also knew that the God was abundantly compassionate, gracious, loving, and kind toward his people.

Knowing that the Lord of all creation can forgive you is astounding! It is humbling, and it provokes a tender willingness to be a better person. Sin is a serious issue, but God wants us to know that he openly forgives, heals sin's wounds, and fosters a broad, new understanding of the depths of the love of Christ within each person who asks. Jesus' compassion is what changes our hearts to want to do good, and to live in peace with him as we walk through life.

God, I forgive everyone who has hurt me, and I ask you to forgive me where I've hurt you and others. Please forgive me and free my heart. Thank you for your kindness.

LEADING THE FLOCK

Be shepherds of God's flock that is under your care,
watching over them—not because you must, but because
you are willing, as God wants you to be; not pursuing
dishonest gain, but eager to serve; not lording it over
those entrusted to you, but being examples to the flock.
And when the Chief Shepherd appears, you will receive the
crown of glory that will never fade away.
1 PETER 5:2-4 NIV

You have joined the teaching profession not only because you care about information or training but because you care about people. The thing that makes you an excellent teacher is that you value people and you want them to be better for having been in your class.

In teaching, you assume the role of leadership. You may very well be the first leader some students have ever believed cared for them on an individual level. Your position is remarkable, and the Lord will give you courage and stamina to live according to his pattern for leadership. There is reward ahead for your hard work—either here on earth when a former student comes to thank you, or in heaven when you are recognized by God.

Lord, please let me follow your pattern of leadership. I want to bless you and the students you have placed in my care.

THE PRINCIPAL'S OFFICE

Because of my integrity you uphold me
and set me in your presence forever.
PSALM 41:12 NIV

Sooner or later, one of your students will get sent to the principal's office. It isn't for good behavior that they receive the honor of this special meeting. Rather, it usually happens as the result of an escalation of poor conduct that has exceeded acceptable classroom limits.

Isn't it wonderful that when God sends you into his presence it is a reward? Psalm 41 states that God will keep you standing as you pass through life here on the earth because you have chosen integrity. It also says that God has not deemed this present reward enough to bless you for your faithful obedience: he will seat you near himself in heaven where you can peacefully enjoy his presence.

Lord, thank you for your promises. Please help and encourage me as I choose to journey with you in integrity. I love you and am deeply grateful that your presence is a place of great reward.

FULLY ACCEPTED

Before he made the world, God chose us to be his very own through what Christ would do for us; he decided then to make us holy in his eyes, without a single fault—we who stand before him covered with his love.

EPHESIANS 1:4 TLB

God has chosen you to be his. He measures you not by your imperfections but by the righteousness of Christ. If God sees you this way, you should too. God accepts you, loves you, and forgives you. He gives you a new beginning and calls you faithful because you trust him. Yes, God chose you to live a fully accepted life.

As a child accepted by God, you know how to love and accept others. This is one of the many reasons the entire field of teaching is blessed when believers fill the posts. A loving, accepting teacher blesses children, who can then easily come to God without distrust. Certainly your role in their lives is vital.

Daddy, thank you for choosing me and for giving me a way to be faultless and holy in your eyes. Thank you for your love that covers me, and for making me a bridge for my students to reach you.

LEAD AND THE REST WILL FOLLOW

Believe on the Lord Jesus Christ, and you will be saved, you and your household.

ACTS 16:31 NKJV

It is amazing and delightful to consider how highly God values faith. Abraham believed in the Lord, and was declared righteous as a result. When you consider God's faithfulness and choose to believe what he tells you, he will move mountains for you. When you trust him to forgive you and lead you for the rest of your life, your family will choose him as well.

How good our heavenly Father is, that he would not only save you, but also your household! Sitting before you each day are students who have families. As you pray for each of your unsaved family members, remember your students in prayer. God will hear your prayers and will bless their families.

Heavenly Father, thank you for accepting my faith and for moving mountains! Thank you for caring about me and my family, and for working your good will into the lives of those I love. Thanks for placing me in a work role where I can pray for students and families I would not otherwise touch. Please bless them and show them the light of your salvation.

HOPEFUL GROWTH

*Blessed be the God and Father of our Lord Jesus Christ!
According to his great mercy, he has caused us to be born
again to a living hope through the resurrection of Jesus
Christ from the dead.*
1 PETER 1:3 ESV

The words you speak to your students are much like
the hope Jesus has given you. You instruct them day by
day, knowing that what you are giving them provides for
their success in academics and work. As they venture forth,
remembering and using what you have taught them, they
start to enjoy the fruits of your partnership with them. This
produces more hope, and underscores the fact that what they
have learned is lifegiving. They guard their knowledge and
grow in it.

God, in his mercy, has given each believer a much better
hope: a steady, calm assurance that we are forgiven in him.
We live a new life, and we have brighter futures than we can
imagine. As we praise and bless the Lord, we connect with his
living hope, and we better understand the value of it as his
truth grows within us.

**God, I bless and praise you! Thank you for your mercy and
the hope you give me through Jesus' resurrection. I give
you this day to work out, in me, the understanding of hope
in my life. I give you my students, and ask you to help me
respond to their needs in a way that glorifies you.**

BLAMELESS

*Blessed be the God and Father of our Lord Jesus Christ,
who has blessed us in Christ with every spiritual blessing
in the heavenly places, even as he chose us in him before
the foundation of the world, that we should be holy and
blameless before him.*

EPHESIANS 1:3-4 ESV

It is gratifying to know that God wishes to bless you. He
chose you before the world began, offering you Jesus and
rewarding you with a multitude of spiritual blessings for
choosing him.

Jesus makes you blameless; he doesn't point a finger at
you for sin, but instead allows you to grow in righteousness. It
hurts when we mess up, but God's love covers a multitude of
sin. Jesus' direction for you is plain and good. As you discover
and enjoy the overwhelming abundance of God's blessings for
you, you abound and spill those blessings onto people around
you including your students.

**Heavenly Father, you have blessed me with Jesus, and
you have blessed me with every spiritual blessing. I pray
I would discover these gifts and use them for your glory.
Thank you for calling me your child and instructing me in
righteousness and goodness.**

CROWN OF LIFE

Blessed is anyone who endures temptation. Such a one has stood the test and will receive the crown of life that the Lord has promised to those who love him.

JAMES 1:12 NRSV

If you have ever run a long race, or participated in another athletic feat, you know that endurance is the key to your success. You spend time each day practicing and conditioning your heart. You eat differently and you take better care of your body. You give up vices that would hinder your success. Why do you go through all this work? Because you want to finish.

God offers the crown of life to those who endure the test of faith throughout their lives. Because we want to finish well, we put no evil thing before our eyes, we watch our speech, and we guard our hearts. We spend time in God's presence and we read and meditate upon his Word. Why? Because the crown of life is far better than any medal we could receive. We joyfully run the race of life for Jesus and look forward to receiving the crown of life that he has prepared for us to wear, eternally, as our reward.

God, help me to run the race well, and be a good example of grace and endurance for my students. Thank you for growing your goodness inside the hearts of people who draw near to you.

BEING REAL

Confess your sins to each other and pray for each other so that you may be healed. The prayer of a righteous person is powerful and effective.
JAMES 5:16 NIV

The Lord doesn't want us to have skeletons in our closets. He wants us to be open with one other, and faithful to encourage and support each other in life's ups and downs. Through our compassionate prayers for one another, we will change the circumstances of life.

In a time when church members cannot be real with each other, we choose to break the mold. We agree to be real. We also agree to be a safe place for our students to approach when they have problems. If love covers a multitude of sins, our prayers and kindness are certainly cherished by Jesus.

Heavenly Father, I know you want the best for me. Help me to be fully accountable to someone trustworthy. I don't want to be fake and pretend that everything is perfect in my life. Please give me a heart of understanding, so that I will live out this verse in a manner that pleases you and brings refreshing to others and myself.

MAY

Discretion will preserve you;
Understanding will keep you.

Proverbs 2:12 nkjv

BIBLICAL BREAKFAST

Continue in what you have learned and have become convinced of, because you know those from whom you learned it, and how from infancy you have known the Holy Scriptures, which are able to make you wise for salvation through faith in Christ Jesus.

2 TIMOTHY 3:14-15 NIV

All that you learn in the Bible is sustenance for life. As you digest God's Word each morning, the Holy Spirit breathes on the Scripture, telling you its meaning, relevance, and application. When you read the Word, you begin to comprehend God's plan of salvation, how all are accountable to him, and how a life of faith and obedience is truly living. You also understand that a life of doubt and disobedience is not life in any form.

How truly blessed we are to have the Holy Spirit with us and to have the Word of God available to equip and transform us. As we partake in the spiritual meal of Scripture reading, we recognize our inherent accountability to live a fulfilled life of salvation and unity with God. Our first step of obedience is faith, and our second is to follow.

Holy Spirit, please help me to read and understand my Bible today. Speak to my heart through today's Word, and give me understanding that illuminates my soul. Then, I will continue in what I have learned by integrating it into my life as a worker that needs not be ashamed.

MOLDED BY MERCY

Don't get angry.
Don't be upset; it only leads to trouble.
PSALM 37:8 NCV

It's all about mercy: covering injustices with love and forgiveness, rather than letting injustice gnaw on you from the inside. You don't drink poison expecting another person to suffer! Likewise, you don't hold a grudge, hoping someone will get the gist of your angst and become righteous in your estimation. Mercy solves that.

Jesus was a perfect example of how mercy covers sin and transforms people. Because God gives us mercy, we can give it to others. Because he set us free, we set others free. You are a beacon of hope and grace to every face you see in your classroom. Because you choose to operate in kindness instead of anger, your students can have inner peace and mercy to pass on to others.

God, help me to remember the mercy you have lavished on me, so I can respond by lavishing it on others. I know this isn't about rules; it's about valuing people. Guide me in your mercy and help me to express love over judgment.

SEASONS OF TRIAL

*Don't worry about anything; instead, pray about
everything. Tell God what you need, and thank him for all
he has done. Then you will experience God's peace, which
exceeds anything we can understand. His peace will guard
your hearts and minds as you live in Christ Jesus.*

PHILIPPIANS 4:6-7 NLT

Jesus told us before he ascended to heaven that although
this world is full of troubles, he has overcome it. What joy this
gives us in seasons of trial! We have no fear in the face of
turmoil, because nothing is greater than our Savior.

In spending genuine, intimate time with Jesus, you
experience growing levels of peace, and achieve breakthrough
in the various areas of your work and personal life. Come to
him in humility and gratitude. Lay out your heart's concerns.
You can be sure that as you persist in prayer, your peace will
overflow and your heart will be protected by his presence and
love. When you give your grief to God, it no longer belongs to
you, it becomes his property, and he will take care of it.

**Daddy, you are so good! Please give me your presence
and your peace. I have a whole bunch of stuff on my heart,
and it starts like this…**

YOUR UNIQUE OPPORTUNITIES

Each of you should use whatever gift you have received to serve others, as faithful stewards of God's grace in its various forms.
1 PETER 4:10 NIV

It can be deflating to experience struggle and failure in areas where we think we should thrive. Even as we cheer others' victories on with open hearts, we can, at times, sense self-disappointment at not having mastered the same degree of excellence.

We are not called to compare ourselves to others. We shouldn't fret over imperfections or the slowness of our progress in comparison to those who are enjoying accolades. Rather, we are to keep in step with Christ, focusing on what unique opportunities he has set before us. We are accountable for these things, not for how we compare to others.

Jesus, thank you for my gifts! Help me to focus on you instead of distractions. Help me to be the very best at who you have created me to be. Illuminate the path you have chosen specifically for me.

SHOWERED WITH GRACE

God is so rich in mercy, and he loved us so much, that even though we were dead because of our sins, he gave us life when he raised Christ from the dead. (It is only by God's grace that you have been saved!) God saved you by his grace when you believed. And you can't take credit for this; it is a gift from God. Salvation is not a reward for the good things we have done, so none of us can boast about it.

EPHESIANS 2:4-5, 8-9 NLT

God loved us in our fallen state and wanted to show us mercy. He did this by showering grace on us—life-giving grace! Because grace is so important, God wanted to give us a front row seat to see and understand it. He seated us beside Jesus Christ, as a coheir and fellow child of God.

We didn't deserve it; it was kindness. Now, we have access to his intimacy and grace. Why is this so important to us? Because grace is what saved us, and when we get in touch with it, we can better understand God's kindness and mercy. When we understand his love, we can fully enjoy it.

God, thank you for your grace and compassion that brought Jesus to the cross, and me to your throne room. I love you so much! Please give me free understanding of your mercy and grace, so that I can understand and revel in your love, as you have desired. I know I need this every day!

A BETTER GLORY

He will take our weak mortal bodies and change them into glorious bodies like his own, using the same power with which he will bring everything under his control.

PHILIPPIANS 3:21 NLT

This is the promise God gives to his people: he will change them from current glory to a better one; eternal and far beyond our comprehension or the desires we could dream. We can see this pattern in so much of what God does with us. Consider, for instance, the tree that produces apples bearing more seed potential than the land can hold.

Certainly, this example illustrates God's great trade-up program, which permeates many facets of the physical and spiritual world. Likewise, we experience the great trade-up when we trust Jesus in faith, and he counts it all as righteousness. When we submit to change, God replaces the old with a much better version. It is a relief and joy to know that God's love has power to change.

Jesus, I love you. Thank you for upgrades. I don't always understand change, but I choose to trade my worries for your wonder. Your perspective is healthy and your reward is unsurpassable.

JESUS IS NOT DONE

I am confident of this very thing, that He who began a good work in you will perfect it until the day of Christ Jesus.

PHILIPPIANS 1:6 NASB

What a blessing it is to know that Jesus is not done with us; his certain guidance and help inspires our steady confidence. When we can let go of our regrets and fears, and remember that Jesus is in control and only asks our trust and obedience, we live freely. We prosper in our growth.

Imagine what it would be like if your students were required to create their own outcomes and curriculum. What an impossible thought! These students would not thrive. Moreover, they would constantly worry about failure. It would become a frustrating, annoying, and fearful experience. Thankfully, this is not the way education works for us. Like your students, you are not required to be transformed by your own devices. Instead, you rely solely upon Jesus' power. When you partner with Jesus in faith, trusting and obeying him, you confidently follow his plan, knowing that all will be well for you.

Jesus, thank you for covering my life with your love and grace! I am so glad you have a plan, and you wrote it down in your book. I'm grateful you are faithful to complete the work of salvation you have begun in my life.

PRAY FOR THE BODY

I have not stopped giving thanks to God for you.
I always remember you in my prayers.
EPHESIANS 1:16 NCV

Paul thanked God for the Christians due to a specific reason, and he prayed for them for a specific purpose. Paul thanked God because he recognized two important facts. First, he knew he was called to live in a way that would make people praise God. Second, he knew later Jesus-followers would have that same calling. You have that calling.

Paul prayed for the body of Christ so we would succeed, collectively and individually. As we know God better, we are enlightened in the hope of our inheritance. We press on in faith, knowing that God has already empowered us and crushed the enemy under our feet. We are able and free to glorify God so people can see and praise him as well.

God, thank you for the Church. Thank you for the glory that you get when people praise you. Please give your children wisdom and revelation, enlightenment, and an intimacy with you that helps us glorify you on the earth.

WILLING INTEGRITY

I know, my God, that you test the heart and are pleased with integrity. All these things I have given willingly and with honest intent. And now I have seen with joy how willingly your people who are here have given to you.
1 CHRONICLES 29:17 NIV

This verse was part of the prayer David spoke to the Lord at the coronation of his son, Solomon. He was so grateful to God. He worshiped and glorified him, praised him and thanked him. The reward David received for his integrity was that he saw the people of his kingdom willingly offer themselves to God as well.

Because you conduct your heart and your day in willing uprightness, your students—even the stubborn ones—will be transformed as they view your behavior. You have a reward for the impact you have made on the people God puts under your authority. Take heart, although it is often tested at school, Jesus will bless your willing integrity!

God, you are the standard of integrity. Please help me to pass the tests you put before me, so that the people who look to me for answers and find a good role model for integrity. I want to bless you and lead others in your ways.

TESTIMONY OF JESUS

I thank God because in Christ you have been made rich in every way, in all your speaking and in all your knowledge.
1 CORINTHIANS 1:5 NCV

When God speaks to our hearts, every good thing flourishes. As we open our hearts to his Word, he transforms them, filling them with his truth, and strengthening them with Scripture that he later brings to our remembrance. So many times this has been the saving grace that has kept us from saying or doing the wrong thing in class, before other teachers, or in the presence of parents.

How good it is to know that in seeking after Jesus with all of our hearts, we submit our lives to become testimonies of Jesus and his grace. This is why people ask us about Jesus. This is why they might hold to a standard we evoke. Although it may be difficult to see each day, people do learn what we know and believe by watching the way we carry ourselves. Jesus has spoken into our hearts, and his word does not return void. Take courage in the fact that you are enriching lives with your words and actions.

God, please help me to be tender in my heart toward you, hungry for your Word, and diligent in your ways. I love you, Lord, and I am grateful, in advance, that you are making my heart richer every day.

YOUR TRUE IDENTITY

If anyone is in Christ, he is a new creation. The old has passed away; behold, the new has come.

1 CORINTHIANS 5:17 ESV

What great confidence we have when we know just who we are in Christ! Oh, the benefits and assurance we possess in being grounded in our heavenly Father's advocacy for us. We cannot be separated from his love. When we said yes to Jesus, we awakened our true identity: an identity infinitely grander than we could have imagined.

Now that you live in your new identity, your heavenly Father gazes upon you and sees the righteousness of Christ. God's heart is *for* you and he encompasses you with his favor. This favor is like a shield—nothing can penetrate it. Abide with Christ. Enjoy who he is and who he has made you to be.

Heavenly Father, you call me righteous and you have drawn me to intimacy. Please help me to receive this intimacy, to read your Word, and to join in worshiping you with other believers. Strengthen me, so that I can walk in my correct identity.

FAITHFUL REDEMPTION

I will not remove from him my steadfast love,
or be false to my faithfulness.

PSALM 89:33 NRSV

This verse was written by David to record God's promise to love and preserve his family line. It captures God's faithful heart of love. Israel did sin after God's promise was made. They made some huge errors, and they paid for their mistakes. All the while, God waited for them to come back, and he loved them according to his promise. Eventually, Christ was born from the line of David, and all of the followers of God saw their redemption.

Do you feel that you have done something that warrants punishment or God's withdrawal? Jesus paid for every sin on the cross. He is standing beside you, true to his faithfulness; dusting off your knees, holding you tightly, and helping you get on your feet again. Do not let sin stand between you and God, but come to him and receive cleansing and freedom.

Father God, please help me to be free of whatever has tried to hinder my understanding and my hope in living and being loved freely by you. Thank you for your faithfulness and love.

CONTAGIOUS KINDNESS

I will tell of the kindnesses of the LORD,
the deeds for which he is to be praised,
according to all the LORD has done for us…
according to his compassion and many kindnesses.

ISAIAH 63:7 NIV

Early in life, many of us learned that Jesus loves us. We have learned that he is mighty, and that his righteousness requires our own. But what happens when we recognize his kindness? It is in the moment we realize that Jesus has stepped into our personal situation that our spirits quicken in love and gratitude toward him. A new understanding of his omnipotence is born; it makes us want to shout and sing!

Our Father in heaven, who loves us, joyfully accepts this praise. He shows himself in the tender compassion of his response to our needs and desires. May your day be filled with the blessings of the Lord: his tender care, his compassion through you, and his abounding encouragement from others.

God, I thank and praise you because you are kind. You have created everything, and you have created me to praise you. Help me share your kindness with people today.

JESUS IS LORD

If you declare with your mouth, "Jesus is Lord," and
believe in your heart that God raised him from the dead,
you will be saved.

ROMANS 10:9 NIV

"I have read my assignment."
"This really is my paper."
"I didn't take his lunch."

We hear them all the time: declarations and promises. And
we spend a good portion of each day sorting out which are
truthful and which are not.

Isn't it a pleasant relief to know that Jesus speaks only the
truth and always stands by his Word? Jesus blesses us, now
and forever, for trusting his promises and walking alongside
him in faith. Let us rest in this truth as we train our students to
be accountable as well.

**Jesus, thank you for paying the price to free me from lies
and false promises. I am blessed to have your truth with
me, always. Please help me to grow in the ability to teach
students to keep their promises.**

EXPECTANT ENDINGS

We are citizens of heaven, where the Lord Jesus Christ lives. And we eagerly wait for him to return as our savior.
PHILIPPIANS 3:20 NLT

Come April and May, it begins. The countdown is ticking, the flowers are blooming, and the wind blows in gusts of a well-known truth: the last day of school is coming. Think of the bubbling joy of the students, especially those that have come a long way from that sticky August day not even knowing how to read. We all look forward to when the last bell rings and the books are closed. Summer is here and with it the green grass, open skies, long days of sunshine, and the feeling of freedom.

How much more are we to anticipate the well-known truth that Jesus is going to return! Armed with an eternal mindset that we belong with Christ in heaven, the temporary fights of this world pale in comparison to our eternal home. Keep the last day at the forefront of your mind; keep the picture of your eternal home taped to your wall. Imagine the summer-like beauty of that day: the glorious light of our Savior, freedom from sin. How can you remind yourself of this truth today? Take a moment to pray for that end-of-year joy to well up inside of you at the assurance of his return.

Jesus, I look forward to eternity with you! Help me to keep my eyes focused on your return.

YOU ARE NEEDED

In everything I showed you that by working hard in this manner you must help the weak.
ACTS 20:35 NASB

It isn't always easy to help the weak. Sometimes people don't see where they fail, or they prefer the excuse to the cure. Sometimes they just need to get over their fear of success. If the hurdle seems too difficult, a select few might even make enough trouble to deter the efforts of those that are willing to help them.

Don't give up. You are the salt of the earth. As long as you are able, giving help to others is crucial, and it is very precious to the Lord. Every bit of what you do will be rewarded in heaven. Hold to the truth and keep pressing forward. God loves you, and he loves your servant heart.

Jesus, thank you for encouraging my helpfulness. Thank you for watching me and guiding me as I walk in your compassion. I am big enough, with you, for the work set before me. I know you are planting a crop of helpfulness so we can reap a harvest of victory.

NOT JUST WISHFUL THINKING

In hope we have been saved, but hope that is seen is not hope; for who hopes for what he already sees? But if we hope for what we do not see, with perseverance we wait eagerly for it.

ROMANS 8:24-25 NASB

"Did you do well on the quiz?"
"I hope so. My grade really needs it!"

Students sometimes think of hope as little more than wishing for a favorable option. Granted, if they are unsure of their chances, it seems this might be their only type of hope. The hope of Jesus is sure. The reason we hope is that we cannot see the result of our faith with physical eyes yet. The reason we are sure about this, not just wishing in advance, is that Jesus is trustworthy.

Knowing Jesus helps us to have hope as we abide in him, awaiting the manifestation of his glory. We are so eager to see the King! This hope carries us through life's storms like proper studying can carry a student through quiz day.

Lord, thank you for taking care of things unseen, so that I can trust you and enjoy the anticipation of your promises. I trust you to guide me and wait eagerly for you.

BEFORE, NOW, AND ALWAYS

Jesus Christ is the same yesterday and today and forever.
HEBREWS 13:8 NASB

God never changes. He has never given up on you, held back from you, or stopped loving you. He constantly holds his dreams for your good future and well-being in his heart. He continually intercedes for you with the Father.

Jesus has never gone back on a promise, and he is not about to do so now. The world may change; your Lord will not. Throughout the ages, Jesus has always been, and will be, the same.

Jesus, I bless your name! Thank you for not changing, or pulling out the rug from under me. Knowing that you are true gives me great comfort and security. Help me to foster this at school so that my students know I am reliable, fair, and sincere, showing love to each person, and living an honorable life.

GODLY TASKS

Keep your conduct among the Gentiles honorable, so that when they speak against you as evildoers, they may see your good deeds and glorify God on the day of visitation.
1 PETER 2:12 ESV

Respect, esteem, dignity, and distinction: these are all words one might use to define honor. At work, you are given sets of tasks to complete, and among them are tasks set for you by God. Love everyone, choose joy, make and keep peace, exercise patience with everyone, be kind at all times, be wholesome and acceptable in your conduct and thoughts, be loyal, and keep yourself in control.

Frankly, your job description encompasses many of these, but cannot incorporate all of them. That is why you, a worker of Jesus, are the salt and light of the earth. It's why the world of education needs you. It's why unbelievers near you will honor you and glorify God.

God, I know this isn't just a to-do list. It is fruit that your nearness produces in my life. Help me draw near to you so that I can grow in this fruit as a witness of your goodness to others.

DREAMS OF YOUR HEART

Know therefore that the LORD your God is God; he is the faithful God, keeping his covenant of love to a thousand generations of those who love him and keep his commandments.

DEUTERONOMY 7:9 NIV

God is love. His kindness is so overwhelming that he gives a one-thousand-generation blessing to trump anything silly our generations might do. He then wipes our slates clean through Jesus, ensuring certain victory over whatever might beset us. His good intentions for us are so grand and so woven into our hearts that when we recognize them, we call them our dreams.

The author of your life writes dreams on your heart, and if you live faithfully with him, you will find rich fulfillment. It's a partnership of faith with the one who loves you and keeps his covenant with you.

God, you love me with an everlasting love. Let this love cause me to follow the dreams that you have placed in my heart.

BURDEN OF TRUTH

Let the elders who rule well be considered worthy of double honor, especially those who labor in preaching and teaching.
1 TIMOTHY 5:17 ESV

You can see the work Jesu did in teaching, especially throughout the gospels. He understands the burden of truth that teachers carry. You have a lot on your plate—training in understanding for righteous use of truth, inspiration to produce from what is learned, and motivation to take action with that inspiration and understanding.

You are teaching not only the students before you, but also the invisible audience of their friends, families, and future generations. Because Jesus has enlightened your perspective, you teach not only math and science, but also God's kingdom and kindness in what you do. Because you teach, someone in your classroom is going to want to teach too. What a profound and uplifting thought!

God, give me the ability to share what you give me to teach in a way that glorifies you and touches hearts. Help me to instruct people, not topics, even on the hard days. Help me see you working through and for me, encouraging, blessing, and cheering me on.

HARMONIZED WITH CHRIST

May the God of endurance and encouragement grant you to live in such harmony with one another, in accord with Christ Jesus, that together you may with one voice glorify the God and Father of our Lord Jesus Christ. Therefore welcome one another as Christ has welcomed you, for the glory of God

ROMANS 15:5-7 ESV

The apostle Paul was an incredible intercessor. He prayed thoughtfully, with wisdom and understanding. He knew that God's intention is that we get along, together, and glorify him in unity. Unity requires daily endurance and encouragement.

At work, you will run into people with different agendas, and not all of the agendas are helpful. Children don't even apologize for this! But you are filled with the Holy Spirit and his agenda is 100% good. He continually pours endurance and encouragement into your soul, if you will receive it. You will co-labor with him to create peace and unity wherever you have been given authority. What a refreshing joy! God is interested in keeping you in his perfect peace today and to use you to breed a cooperative spirit at work.

God, thank you for your encouragement! You know my environment, and you know my own ways. Please walk with me today, and help me to be open to your constant revelation. Help students to feel the difference of your goodness and nearness to their situation. Help me to be a vessel of your goodness and cooperation.

STORED FOR YOU

One thing I have desired of the LORD,
that will I seek:
that I may dwell in the house of the LORD
all the days of my life
to behold the beauty of the LORD,
and to inquire in His temple.

PSALM 27:4 NKJV

It is a great and awesome adventure that we choose when we enter into relationship with our heavenly Father. To behold the beauty of the Lord is like continually unraveling a mystery that never will end. Like Moses in days of old, we consider ourselves honored to witness and wonder over the splendor of the glory of God. His beauty is infinite!

Sometimes, we pause to ponder the unfathomable things our heavenly Lord lovingly desires for us. We try to imagine what he has in store, even on this earth. What an honor, privilege, and blessing to be loved by the King of all kings, who knows all things and invites us into his revelation!

Heavenly Father, I am honored to call you my King and my God. To rest in your presence, gaze on your beauty, and meditate upon your love is the fulfillment of my every desire.

THE ADVANTAGE OF LISTENING

Pay attention to my wisdom;
listen carefully to my wise counsel.
Then you will show discernment;
and your lips will express what you've learned.
PROVERBS 5:1-2 NLT

As we get older, we joke that our parents seem to have grown wiser! But we know the truth; the change has more likely happened to us, than to their intellect. The positions of our hearts have finally softened and changed.

We teach students to honor people and value their instruction. We know that if they are obedient to our words, they will grasp opportunities to sidestep many of the hardships we have endured. In this way, the next generation may stand on the platform of our achievements, taking advantage of the possibility that they may go further than we could have ever imagined in past generations or circumstances.

God, thank you for the tender, learning hearts of children. Help me to impress upon them the virtue of honoring and listening to the people who can help them soar above the weather. Help me, too, to give them wings.

EXPERIENCING WISDOM

*People who work for peace in a peaceful way plant
a good crop of right-living.*
JAMES 3:18 NCV

Helpfulness is an expression of wisdom. God's wisdom
is first pure, then peaceful, gentle, and easy to please. It is
helpful, honest, and fair, and works for the good of others.
Wisdom in motion is the kind of helpfulness described in this
verse and it is exactly what every teacher wishes students
would adopt.

Fortunately, most students do pick up a lot of what they
learn from your choices and behaviors. When you choose
helpfulness according to wisdom, peace, gentleness,
and an easy-going nature, you displace the jealousy and
selfishness that could have interfered with wholesome learning
experiences for your students. Thanks to you, your classroom
gets a taste of God's wisdom every day. What a blessing this
is, and what an inheritance of demeanor for your students!

**God, please be with me each day, showing me the choices
of wisdom I have before me. Please help me to explore
your wisdom more deeply, and to integrate what I learn
into my daily life.**

COLLECTIVE HONESTY

Putting away falsehood, let all of us speak the truth to our neighbors, for we are members of one another.
EPHESIANS 4:25 NRSV

Sometimes, we seek peace at the expense of truth when we see people we love doing things that might hurt them. It makes for awkward circumstances: a lie or avoidance becomes a few lies or increased busyness. We avoid contact, hoping that waters will calm, excusing ourselves from situations. We are glad to assume that others will figure out the tough things of life without our help. However, we know in our hearts that it shouldn't be that way.

Have you ever been in a jam of that sort and been rescued from it by the truthful love of a person who stepped in and saved the situation? At the end of the day, the parties involved resolved that they loved each other, and were each worth the honesty they were afforded. Every one of us is of great value to God and deserves to be treated with respect and honor.

God, help me to have the courage to stand up in truth where you desire it. I know you are the truth, so it is in my nature to want truth to rule my life as well.

RIGHTFUL ESTEEM

Show respect for all people: Love the brothers and sisters of God's family, respect God, honor the king.
1 PETER 2:17 NCV

As instructors, we each teach curriculum according to state standards. We report student progress and conduct, and we confess we spend a certain amount of time with people we wouldn't choose for ourselves. Education can be its own lesson, can it not? In this lesson, we earn a special grace that holds the capacity to impact all areas of our lives. We earn the grace of honoring others. Honor is difficult to give when forced but not earned; honor is extraordinarily like love.

When we see people the way God wants us to see them, we see their inherent value, and we esteem their position properly. We value and protect other members of the body of Christ because we, too, are part of his body. We honor those ahead of us in rank because Christ, the head of the church, tells us to do so. If we struggle with honor, we should take the issue to Jesus, the ruler of all. He gives us wholesome attitudes.

Father, thank you for the fresh perspective that you offer. Please show me if you would like me to consider a different attitude regarding honor toward a particular person. I will listen to you and adopt your opinion, because I trust your Word.

A CLEAN SLATE

Sin shall no longer be your master, because you are not under the law, but under grace.

ROMANS 6:14 NIV

Have you ever considered the paradigm shift Jesus ushered in with the new covenant? It is quite incredible. If you believe in Jesus, you are a new creation, and your past no longer has a hold on you. You have a clean slate, a fresh start. You aren't perfect on your own, of course. Rather, Jesus is perfecting you. He died for all. This is a covenant for everyone.

As we renew our minds in the Word, we learn life isn't about the rules; it's about Jesus. It is about loving him so much that the things that once mastered us no longer have the power to do so. Jesus empowers us to overcome. As we abide in him, we learn that he is not a taskmaster. Rather, he has given us two simple commandments: to love God, and to love others. We walk in the freedom and grace God gives us, knowing the Holy Spirit is gracious to joyfully guide us in all our ways.

God, you are righteous and good! Thank you for the grace to live a full and free life. I accept your easy yoke of love and kindness. Help me to walk in your grace today.

FATHERLY ACCEPTANCE

"The Father gives me the people who are mine. Every one of them will come to me, and I will always accept them."
JOHN 6:37 NCV

If we feel inadequate or weak, we know it is time to come to the heavenly Father for some spiritual rest. The Father has boundless love for you and offers you refreshment as you sit at his feet as an accepted child. You cannot be inadequate to your heavenly Father. He gazes at you through the cross of Christ and sees you as perfect—washed and clean. You are his child. You are fully accepted in Jesus, by the will of your Father, who will not be dissuaded.

What an amazing love—that we are accepted without reservation! Such love inspires confidence, refreshment, and a burning desire to respond in like manner. God is our Father and our accepting friend. Hallelujah!

Jesus, I need you. I'm tired, and sometimes I don't even accept myself. But you know me, and you have a better plan for me than I can imagine. Show me your love for me, God, and remind me what it is to be accepted, so I can receive it and give it to others.

HAND IT OVER

The generous will themselves be blessed
for they share their food with the poor.
PROVERBS 22:9 NIV

It is in every human's spiritual DNA to give because we are made in the image of the premier giver. We see encouragement and modeling for giving repeatedly in the Bible. God loved us so much that *he* gave! Even nonbelievers give, recognizing the law of sowing and reaping. Because God cares for the poor, he will bless those who give.

We have a great advantage in the area of giving because God lives in us, filling our hearts with conviction and compassion to help. We please him when we act upon that love. When we tithe, God invites us to test his goodness, because he promises to bless us beyond overflowing. When we give offerings, we build our communities, and everyone flourishes. When we give to the poor, sharing our food and meeting their needs, we lend to the Lord who generously repays.

God, please give me a greater passion for giving and a special heart for the poor so I can serve you by serving those most in need. I am opening my eyes to see people, Lord. Please help me cross paths with the ones you want to help, even in my classroom.

WALKING BESIDE THE MASTER

The LORD is good to those whose hope is in him,
to the one who seeks him.
LAMENTATIONS 3:25 NIV

Have you ever wondered what it was like to be a disciple of Jesus? Walking alongside him, witnessing miracle after miracle. Watching him calm the wild, stormy seas by declaring peace. Seeing a dead man come to life after his family and friends had mourned him for four days. The confidence you would have carried would be this: that anything coming against you would be taken care of by your big brother.

Jesus was the perfect representation of the heavenly Father. With this in mind, we carry within us a confidence that as we go through the trials of any kind, our heavenly Father waits for each of us to call upon him. He will give us peace in the middle of the storm. He will heal our broken hearts. All we ever need to do is call on him. He rewards those who diligently seek after him.

Heavenly Father, thank you for loving me. Thank you for rewarding those who diligently seek you. Thank you for breaking me free from doubt to enjoy your hope that creates change in my heart.

JUNE

You were once darkness,
but now you are light in the Lord.

Live as children of light.

Ephesians 5:8 niv

GOOD REASONS

The Spirit of the LORD shall rest upon Him,
The Spirit of wisdom and understanding,
The Spirit of counsel and might,
The Spirit of knowledge and of the fear of the LORD.
ISAIAH 11:2 NKJV

Understanding isn't so much about knowing what to do as it is about knowing what makes that action wise. For every commandment God ever gave, there is a reason. Here is a common example. God tells us not to kill other people. Why? Because he creates life. It is our God-given drive to support life; violating that opposes our God-given nature and destroys his image in another human being. It is a crushing thought.

Just as there are reasons for everything God does and commands regarding his creation, there are reasons for everything you teach. Some are obvious, while others are obscure. Giving your students the gift of eagerness to understand will help them care about school and will establish their adult lives with purpose and meaning.

God, please give me an understanding heart, so I can bring your keys of successful living to my students in whatever environment I can. Thank you for making me in your image, for loving me, forgiving me, and making me a nurturer of life.

THE TRUE SOURCE

The very essence of your words is truth.
PSALM 119:160 NLT

It is a difficult to teach when we do not agree with the materials before us. Every day, students receive many informational inputs, and not all of them are true or uplifting. Before we look at that lesson plan that we loathe, let's take a moment to consider the wholesomeness of God in his instruction to us.

Truth is the essence of God's words. Essence is translated from the Hebrew word *rash*. *Rash* means "head" or "beginning." In effect, it says God is our head, and he is true. The Word of God, the essence of the Bible, is a detailed expression of our heavenly Father's heart toward us. We have peace in knowing that God is never going to teach us something against his nature. Bring the difficulties of curriculum to him for his peaceful response. His truth sets us free as we wait on him.

Jesus, thank you that you are the source of the truth. As I read your Word, please help me understand how it can be properly applied to my teaching experiences. I want to represent the truth in what I say and do, and give the students in my care a good frame of reference for life.

HIGHWAY OF RIGHTEOUSNESS

They who wait for the LORD shall renew their strength;
they shall mount up with wings like eagles;
they shall run and not be weary;
they shall walk and not faint.

ISAIAH 40:31 ESV

Have you ever followed that little voice that tells you to do something, and found out later it was really good you did? God's words to us come in many forms: a gnawing feeling, a gentle nudge, a warm affirmation. At times, we read our Bibles and know that we are being reminded, in Scripture, of something that needs to happen. These are ways that we hear from the Lord.

When we compare what we think to Scripture and follow his bidding instead of going our own way, our path becomes wide and well lit. It is a highway of righteousness instead of a difficult, bramble-filled path. When faced with our way or God's, we can rest assured that placing ourselves in God's presence is always going to become the choice that bears great fruit.

God, I praise you! Please give me the insight to sit in your presence, wait for your viewpoint, and listen to your guidance. I am willing to wait on you and do things your way instead of my own.

CONFIDENT REQUESTS

This is the confidence that we have toward him, that if we ask anything according to his will he hears us. And if we know that he hears us in whatever we ask, we know that we have the requests that we have asked of him.

1 JOHN 5:14 ESV

It would be hard to understand the confidence of a believer if we couldn't explain it or be given a chance to live it out. John says God gives audience to the requests we make that are in his will. He is indeed intent on granting our requests. So, how do we know God's will, and why would we be drawn to it?

As believers, we love God and obey his commandments. Because loving God and obeying him is a sign that we love each other, we naturally have a desire to excel in this. Our Father's response to us causes our further confidence in him and in his ability to complete his will through each one of us.

God, please give me passion for what moves you! I don't want to live this life unto myself. You have given me a life to live, students to impact, and my portion of the world to transform. Let me leave your legacy for others to inherit and enjoy.

HOME OF THE WISE

Through wisdom a house is built,
and by understanding it is established;
by knowledge the rooms are filled
with all precious and pleasant riches.
A wise man is strong, yes,
a man of knowledge increases strength.

PROVERBS 24:3-5 NKJV

God has a precious gift in you. Although many teachers have the ability to teach, you have a special connection with God that gives you opportunity to dispense wisdom as well. You have access to your heavenly Father, who gives you what you ask to produce an abundant harvest in the fields—your students.

Wisdom is necessary to build a house and keep it running before the baubles of knowledge will have a place to lodge. In other words, when you know what you should do and why, the technical matters of basic education will become of utmost importance.

Father, I praise you because you know all things and you know what matters for me and for my students right now. Please, give me an understanding of the importance of the lessons I am to teach. Show me how these lessons practically apply to my students, so they will naturally want to remember what they need to learn.

FAITH BUILDERS

We never forget your loving deeds as we talk to our God and Father about you, and your strong faith and steady looking forward to the return of our Lord Jesus Christ.
1 Thessalonians 1:3 tlb

Do you remember the teachers who inspired you to teach? Everyone has them: favorites who formed their thoughts on school, education, and careers. The most common thread among these positive enforcers is love. These are the people who changed our habits, opened our minds, and gave us faith to believe in a good future for ourselves. They saw in you what others did not profess to see. They enabled you to foster your gift, and it grew.

As a teacher, you make choices much like those of the faith builders who inspired you. Thank you for shining the inspiring hope of Jesus, who knows all students according to their potential and their very important futures. Jesus is joyful over them and over you.

God, thank you for reminding me how valuable I am in generating hope for the students I teach. Please forgive me if I haven't seen them for who they really are to you. Thank you for making me a faith builder, so they can trust your work in their lives.

SINCERE HEARTS

Who may worship in your sanctuary, LORD?
Who may enter your presence on your holy hill?
Those who lead blameless lives and do what is right,
speaking the truth from sincere hearts.
PSALM 15:1-2 NLT

Honesty seems to be a difficult virtue to preserve. In many instances, we are begged to tell a little white lie, or to ignore an obvious truth. God weighs our hearts, though. He knowingly writes his words upon their fleshy tables.

We can be sure that our hearts will convict or defend us as we learn to walk in step with God each day. What kindness Jesus displays by helping us, from the heart, to choose actions agreeable with truth. As we keep Jesus present in our lives, we feel his pleasure and sanctuary.

God, help me to be sincere in the truth through my thoughts, words, and actions. I choose to keep my mind stayed on you, because I know it pleases you. Keep me in your presence and help me to lead a blameless life.

LEND YOUR RESOURCES

Whoever is generous to the poor lends to the LORD,
and he will repay him for his deed.

PROVERBS 19:17 ESV

When you have just enough to get by, it is a sacrifice to give to others. Sometimes giving takes the form of filling school supply needs; at other times, it is giving to a person who could never repay. The Bible says that if you are generous to the poor, you are actually paying for something God wants covered.

The Lord made the earth an abundant place. Unfortunately, the resources of the earth seem to pool in certain areas. When we have the ability to distribute to drier places, we choose to do what Jesus wants. That's why he will always repay you. You are spending of your limited resources to step up in his unlimited love, making God-like choices to shine in the world.

God, thank you for generosity and for giving me discernment about where to give. Please help me to be effective in meeting needs. Help me to serve the poor and distribute wealth. Give me creative ideas and open the way so that I can work with others to accomplish even more.

A SUCCESSFUL PURSUIT

*Whoever pursues righteousness and love
finds life, prosperity and honor.*
PROVERBS 21:21 NIV

Have you ever noticed how students pay special attention when they know a reward awaits? Sometimes these rewards are extrinsic, like an additional fun activity. Other times they are natural byproducts of success, such as the final product of a 3D art studio, or a fizzing beaker in a chemistry lab.

Today's verse is an example of weighty intrinsic rewards that await people who choose to live a life of moral soundness and compassionate goodwill. God blesses people by telling them about various dynamic connections between our actions and their results. Even unbelievers know that people are honored when they are kind; we are fashioned to respond in this manner. Proverbs is a book full of these dynamics. Take some time to look up definitions for life, prosperity, and honor. These are all blessings God wants to feed you.

God, give me the insight to see that you really do love everyone and that you will bless me for being the translation of that love on the earth. Show me where I can look like you more, on the inside and out.

THE TOUGH STUFF

You are a chosen people, a royal priesthood, a holy nation, God's special possession, that you may declare the praises of him who called you out of darkness into his wonderful light.
1 PETER 2:9 NIV

Depression saps a person's strength. Easy tasks become insurmountable hurdles, roadblocks to future progress. We become self-focused and dwell on pain, rather than isolating opportunities for change and stepping into the victory of forward living.

Instead of forgetting ourselves upon the couch of despair and grief, we may rest in Jesus. At his side, we tackle each dilemma from a place of belonging, worth, and victory. Jesus draws us up out of dark situations swirling about us. They can no longer abate our peace. With Jesus, we work on the tough stuff of this world's troubles that try to rob us of our joy. Earthly trials cannot steal our victory. After all, Jesus is life, and we love life!

Jesus, you are my hallelujah! Thank you for establishing me as a precious, chosen, holy, royal person. I have had difficulty moving forward at times, but you have ordained me for this race. You are the one who strengthens me and calls me by name. I stand because you are my strength.

GOOD BEHAVIOR

You, O Lord, will bless the righteous;
with favor You will surround him as with a shield.
PSALM 5:12 NKJV

When you give kids a treat because they have helped you with a task, or worked well with others, you exemplify the heart of Christ. God sees what is good and rewards it. You aren't showing partiality by rewarding good behavior. Rather, you preserve the hearts of people who choose good intentions, inspiring more of the same behavior from everyone. It is a blessing to be given favor for doing the right thing. You are acting justly.

As Christ followers, we have been given a great head start on getting rewarded for goodness. From the moment of our conversion, we were weighed as righteous in Christ. As we progress in our walk, we recognize the blessings of growing faith and obedience. We see God's great favor toward us as we choose the right paths.

Lord, thank you for blessing me and preserving me in your favor. I am so glad that you have made me the righteousness of Christ and you honor my righteous behavior by giving me favor. Please help me to treat my students the way you treat me!

PITCH AND PRAY

Cast all your anxiety on him, because he cares for you.
PETER 5:7 NRSV

The human heart has a propensity toward worry. What will happen *if* or *when*? Anxiety is like a seed of fear that, when nurtured, fed, and watered, develops into an organism that devours the life-giving promises in God's Word. It is so comforting to know that God provides an antidote, a pesticide of sorts, which will eradicate the paralyzing seedlings of anxiety.

God's plan is two-fold. First, we are to cast. Picture the fisherman with his arm thrown back ready to cast his line into the water. With one giant heave, his bait flies through the air and ultimately sinks deep into the water. In a similar way, we are to fling, hurl, pitch, and sling our anxieties onto Jesus who gladly bears our burden! Second, the Scriptures say that instead of worrying, we are to pray, with thanksgiving. Pitch and pray.

Lord, thank you for caring about me so much. I know that you don't want me to live with fear and anxiety. Help me to make a habit of pitching and praying!

FOCUSED THOUGHTS

You keep him in perfect peace
whose mind is stayed on you,
because he trusts in you.

ISAIAH 26:3 ESV

According to the National Science Foundation, an average person has approximately 50,000 thoughts per day—1.7 thoughts per second. Others say that number is too low, that we have 75,000-100,000 per day. Given those statistics, keeping our minds focused on God seems completely impossible—kind of like herding cats!

What can God mean? Perhaps it is simply to make sure the natural inclination of our minds and hearts is toward God and that the default in every circumstance isn't fear and doubt, but rather complete trust. This is where we find perfect peace.

Lord, I know that you long for me to live with your perfect peace. Help me to keep my mind stayed on you and trust you completely!

LIFE IN ABUNDANCE

He shall receive a blessing from the LORD
and righteousness from the God of his salvation.
PSALM 24:5 NASB

God's intention and desire is to bless people. We are assured of this hundreds of times over in Scripture. The giver is the Lord, the only true and wise God. The recipients are those with clean hands and pure hearts who are committed to walking in truth.

What are the blessings God promises? Are they approval, help, protection, and provision? Certainly those things, but God's definition is grander. He wants his blessings to permeate every area of our lives, from the everyday mundane to a walk with God that is satisfying and fulfilling. And what of the second part of the verse? We are given the very righteousness of God and are justified in his eyes. He looks upon us with favor. This is the ultimate of all blessings!

Lord, thank you for granting me your righteousness. Help me to keep my heart pure before you. I receive your many blessings so that I may be a channel of blessing to the world.

ACTION AND ATTITUDE

*Religion that is pure and undefiled before God, the Father,
is this: to care for orphans and widows in their distress, and
to keep oneself unstained by the world.*

JAMES 1:27

What kind of religion is acceptable to God as pure
and faultless? Is it found in public displays of worship and
devotion, or more in the sequestered quietness of one's
prayer closet? Perhaps both. True religion is both an action
and an attitude. Caring for the orphan and widow—those in
real need—is evidence of a work of God in the heart. Showing
kindness and care to the hurting is a visible deed. The attitude
that gives birth to such actions is one of purity, devotion, and
separation unto God.

Simply put, serve the needy with a clean heart. We aren't
working hard to gain God's approval; we already have it as we
simply love and care for the needy and stay unblemished by
the world.

**Lord, give me greater capacity to love and care for others.
As I navigate through this messy world, give me a heart of
purity that remains unstained.**

STAGES OF LIFE

There is a time for everything and everything on earth has its special season.

ECCLESIASTES 3:1 NCV

Time can be our biggest enemy and our greatest ally. The lack of it can motivate us toward accomplishment, and in the process, prove to be our friend. Time can speed by like a whirlwind during times of joy or drag along agonizingly in times of struggle. Ecclesiastes addresses the shifting stages of life and encourages us to accept each phase as from the hand of God.

Are you in a season of joy and satisfaction? Love it! Flourish in it! Give it your all! Perhaps you are in a season of difficulty that is weighing you down. Remember, God is present in those moments as well. The Lord has made everything beautiful in its time. All things are not beautiful in life, but he promises to turn them into good at exactly the right time.

Lord, thank you for the varying seasons. They are beautiful in nature and beautiful in my life. Help me relish the joys, and trust you through the valleys!

THE VALUE OF CHILDREN

"Let the little children come to me and do not forbid them;
for of such is the Kingdom of God."

MATTHEW 19:14 NKJV

A mother's love for her child is unique and irreplaceable. From the moment she lays eyes on her precious infant to her last breath, her heart remains captured. Jesus loved children with an even greater love, although his disciples did not understand it and even scolded the parents for bothering him. "Don't chase away the kids," Jesus responded. "Let them come to me. Don't you realize that the kingdom of God belongs to those like them?"

What are children like? They are innocent, trusting, authentic, simple, loving, easily delighted, and much more. They can lead us by example if we allow them to. And yet, Jesus entrusted these treasures into our care, encouraging us to be like them. What a privilege we have in nurturing, teaching, and guiding those in whom God's heart delights.

Thank you for the delightful gift of children. Help me as I cherish and guide those under my care. Help me to respond to you in the same way that these children respond to life.

MOVED BY COMPASSION

Praise be to the God and Father of our Lord Jesus Christ, the Father of compassion and the God of all comfort.

2 CORINTHIANS 1:3 NIV

A little girl entered her school classroom visibly unhappy and disgruntled. It would be impossible to know the reason, but her feelings were obvious. She squeezed herself into a small storage area to comfort herself and no amount of teacher's coaxing could persuade her to emerge. After a bit of time passed, a little friend approached, plopped on the floor alongside her, touching her gently. There were a few quiet words, but after a time, Miss Unhappy's disposition began to change and before long, she was participating in the classroom's activities. That's what compassion can do.

Psalm 86:15 tells us that God is compassionate, gracious, slow to anger, and abounding in love and faithfulness. Christ, the express image of his father, showed us how that looks. He wept at Lazarus' tomb when he saw the sorrow of the bereaved. He was moved with compassion when the suffering crowds sought healing. Compassion is the heart of God, and because of his presence in our lives, it is ours as well.

Praise be to you, God! Thank you for the compassion you feel for your children. Help me exhibit the same as I love and teach those under my care.

YOU CAN DO IT

I can do everything through Christ, who gives me strength.
PHILIPPIANS 4:13 NLT

Public speaking was terrifying for this young student. Shy by nature, unsure of herself, and anything but confident, speaking in front of a group was formidable. The professor had suggested she give her speech to the whole student body during chapel hour. How could she possibly do it, yet how could she possibly decline? The topic? Philippians 4:13.

Sometimes God puts before us opportunities that seem too difficult. Paul knew all about that. God had commissioned him to share the best news on earth, and Paul was passionate about doing it. But he encountered hardships in the process. Earlier in the chapter, he stated that through it all, he had learned to be content in whatever circumstances he faced. He could live on almost nothing or with everything; he could live with a full stomach or hunger, with plenty or little. God supplied the strength he needed, so he could do it all! God will do the same for you.

Thank you, Lord, for the wonderful promise of your strength to do anything you ask me to do. I can be bold and say confidently—I can do all things!

THE COMMAND FOR COURAGE

Keep alert, stand firm in your faith, be courageous,
be strong. Let all that you do be done in love.

1 Corinthians 16:13-14 NRSV

The four imperatives in this verse sound militant and forceful as though speaking to a soldier in battle! Why are we being commanded to be watchful, to stand firm, to be courageous and strong? Consider the Corinthians for a moment. Such a divisive group they were, with their squabbling and arguing. They needed to be reminded that there is more to the Christian life than meets the eye. The Corinthians needed to be watchful of the enemy's designs against them and then, with courage, stand firm in their faith, cloaked all the while in love.

Be encouraged to know today that whatever the opposition, you have the authority, power, and courage of the Holy Spirit to stand firm in your faith!

Lord, some days I am so weak. I feel like I'm fighting a losing battle with people and circumstances. Today I'm going to choose to tap into your strength to stand firm. Fill me with your love in all I do.

ASSURED OF GOD'S PRESENCE

"Have I not commanded you? Be strong and courageous. Do not be frightened, and do not be dismayed, for the Lord Your God is with you wherever you go."

JOSHUA 1:9 ESV

One of the most precious promises God gives to his people is the assurance of his presence. Joshua surely needed these words. He had just been commissioned by God as Moses' successor. He had a mighty nation to lead and was feeling the weight of being solely responsible. God graciously encouraged him.

As these words were spoken to Joshua, so they are spoken to us. We may feel alone in our responsibility. We may feel intimidated by the job at hand. But neither of those two assumptions is true. What is true is God's promised presence. So we can be strong and courageous; God is with us wherever we go!

Lord, I'm so thankful for your presence! I acknowledge that you are with me and whatever today holds, you will be there!

MASTERPIECE

We are God's masterpiece. He has created us anew in Christ Jesus, so we can do the good things he planned for us long ago.

EPHESIANS 2:10 NLT

It is said that the Mona Lisa is the masterpiece of all masterpieces. The most famous and discussed of all paintings, her mysterious smile has captured the imagination of generations. Only an extremely gifted artist could produce such a work and only God could give such a gift. The psalmist says that the heavens declare the glory of God, the skies announce what his hands have made. This is the same God who created you, first fashioned you in his image, and then made you new when he became your Savior. You are his masterpiece, reborn from above and made ready to do the good things he planned long ago for you to do.

Be assured that the assignment God has given you today is pointing others to him. Walk out the good life he ordained for you with confidence; the work you are doing is pleasing to God!

Thank you for creating me anew and giving me a special assignment to complete in my journey through life. Help me to exemplify your glory as I walk the life you planned for me.

OUR DELIVERER

The LORD hears his people when they call to him for help.
He rescues them from all their troubles.

PSALM 34:17 NLT

Isn't it wonderful that God invites us to call out for help when we need it? Think of the many people in the world whose false religions compel them to continually seek their god's approval to avoid his wrath. They live in fear that they will be smitten with disease or disaster if their god is displeased. In stark contrast, we have the one true God who, instead of ruling with a rod of iron and demanding perfection, invites us to bring our troubles to him with love and tenderness.

The immensity of the problem is not important. Large or small, life-altering or seemingly insignificant, all qualify. God comes to the rescue; your deliverer is standing by. Call out to him today. He is listening for your voice.

Thank you, Lord, for rescuing me over and over from my troubles. What a wonderful God you are. I call out to you once more, knowing you will hear me and deliver me again.

A BRIGHTER LOCATION

He has delivered us from the power of darkness and conveyed us into the kingdom of the Son of His love.

COLOSSIANS 1:3 NKJV

When we became Christians, a wonderful thing occurred. Christ gave us a clean heart, filled us with himself, and then changed our location. He took us away from where we once lived in darkness and relocated us to his kingdom of light. We were living apart from Christ in a world without hope. The old life represented by sin and hopelessness is behind us and we are now under new leadership represented by the light of holiness, truth, love, and life.

We need to be reminded of our location at times, especially when things get tough and we battle discouragement. The darkness of the old life attempts to cast a shadow over the light. Christ is shining as brightly as ever. Walk away from the gloom and back into the light.

Thank you, Lord, for transferring me from the realm of darkness into the kingdom of your Son. I love my new home, shining with life and love. Help me to live every day as a child of the light.

HIRED BY HIM

Work with enthusiasm, as though you were working for the Lord rather than for people.

EPHESIANS 6:7 NLT

A small boy climbed up on the kitchen counter and had one hand in the cookie jar when his mother walked in. She asked the obvious question, "What are you doing?" Looking sheepish, he quoted Ecclesiastes 9:10: "Whatever your hand finds to do, do it with all your might!" She had taught him well! The little guy certainly understood the words of the Scripture, just not the application!

We are called to do our work with all our might! Even though this passage discusses the relationship between slaves and masters, the application is universal. Paul tells us that the motive for service to a human master should be as if we were serving the Lord Jesus. For today, no matter who we work for, our service should be done enthusiastically because we are really glorifying Christ! The Lord will reward each one of us for the good we do.

Lord, I am encouraged to remember that you are mindful of all of my work. Help me to do it with enthusiasm as unto you!

WALK WITH EACH OTHER

Encourage one another and build each other up,
just as in fact you are doing.
1 Thessalonians 5:11 niv

"Come on! You can do it! One more step!" Her precious little one is learning to walk! Arms outstretched, each tiny step on unsteady legs is a triumph. From toddlerhood to the golden years, everyone is in need of encouragement.

Before Paul admonishes us to encourage one another, he first builds the foundation on which our hope rests. We are children of the day; we do not belong to darkness. Jesus died for, so whether we are awake or asleep, we will live together with him one day. Let's build each other up. Comfort and encourage the disheartened, help the weak, be patient with everyone. As you uplift others, you yourself will be strengthened and helped.

I'm so grateful, Lord, that as you comfort and encourage me, I can in turn do the same for others. I choose to encourage at least one person today!

WORDS OF LIFE

Don't use foul or abusive language. Let everything you say be good and helpful, so that your words will be an encouragement to those who hear them.

EPHESIANS 4:29 NLT

Words have the power to edify or destroy. Perhaps in your youth, you heard statements like: you'll never amount to anything; you'll never be as bright as your sister; why can't you ever do anything right? Such language is debilitating and, if believed, can become self-fulfilling prophecy.

Jesus pinpointed the problem in Matthew 15:18: "The things that come out of a person's mouth come from the heart." The psalmist prayed the solution in Psalm 51:10: "Create in me a clean heart, O God; and renew a right spirit within me." Let's become people whose words are measured by the life they can bring! May our speech be full of encouragement and our words be loving, patient, gentle, and kind.

Thank you, Lord, for reminding me today that the words I use are powerful. Put a watch at the door of my lips that I might not sin against you. May everything I say be good and helpful to others.

WATERED WITH WISDOM

Let my teaching fall on you like rain; let my speech settle like dew. Let my words fall like rain on tender grass, like gentle showers on young plants.

DEUTERONOMY 32:2 NLT

God told Moses to record a song that would serve as a national anthem to ancient Israel. The preamble of the song reminded them that God was their rock—glorious, perfect, just, and faithful. Through the beautiful metaphor of rain and growth, Moses communicated God's message in a way that would be remembered. The words he was about to prophesy were difficult ones. Yet he desired that these words be received like gentle showers falling on vegetation to cause growth and fruitfulness.

Let's attempt a contemporary application. The gentle, life-giving instruction of a loving teacher will settle like dew on young minds. As the rain turns deserts to meadows, so wise words falling on young minds will bring an awakening of understanding. Be encouraged today to know that your work is influential. The tender young plants in your classroom will grow and flourish under your guidance.

Lord, I desire my teaching to be like rain on young plants and my speech settled like dew. Make me an effective communicator with all the love and grace of Jesus.

RIGHT AROUND THE CORNER

It will happen in a moment, in the blink of an eye,
when the last trumpet is blown. For when the trumpet
sounds, those who have died will be raised to live forever.
And we who are living will also be transformed.

1 CORINTHIANS 15:52 NLT

Nothing in this life surpasses the hope of eternal life granted to those who have put their faith in Jesus Christ. Jesus persevered through the darkest days of his life because of the expectation of the joy awaiting him. He could endure; he could disregard the shameful death, as he knew he would soon be seated in a place of honor beside God's throne. Jesus knew that his suffering was temporary, but his glory eternal.

As the trumpet was often used to summon an assembly in the Old Testament, so the trumpet will again sound and in that blink of an eye, all who have died and all who are living will be transformed! Our dying bodies will be become immortal and eternity will begin. The difficulties we face are only temporary. Glory is right around the corner!

Lord, help me keep my eyes on you, the champion who has initiated and is perfecting my faith. Help me to work enthusiastically for you, because I know that nothing I do for you is useless. Thank you for hope!

A UNIFIED FAMILY

Let the teaching of Christ live in you richly. Use all wisdom to teach and instruct each other by singing psalms, hymns, and spiritual songs with thankfulness in your hearts to God.
COLOSSIANS 3:16 NCV

If you've ever read anything about the behavior of the common ant, you can't help but be impressed. The tiny insects live and work together in highly organized societies. Each colony is a close-knit family united toward a common goal of reproducing more of their kind. They communicate with each other and each plays an important role. Proverbs 6:6 tells us to consider the ant's ways and be wise.

The body of Christ should be a unified family—working, worshiping, and teaching one another for the purpose of glorifying God and multiplying his kingdom. Our roles vary: some teach and instruct, others minister through music, and still others serve. But all need to be full of God's Word and overflowing with thanksgiving that pours out in psalms, hymns, and spiritual songs!

Lord, how I love your Word! I am so thankful for the privilege of being a part of your body. Fill my heart with song and give me wisdom as I instruct others.

JULY

Be filled with the knowledge of His will in all spiritual wisdom and understanding, so that you will walk in a manner worthy of the Lord, to please Him in all respects, bearing fruit in every good work and increasing in the knowledge of God.

COLOSSIANS 1:9-10 NASB

STAND TOGETHER

*Exhort one another day by day, so long as it is called today;
lest any one of you be hardened by the deceitfulness of sin.*
HEBREWS 3:13 NRSV

Exhortation can be defined as communication that
emphatically urges someone to do something. Paul did
that in his letter to a group of Christians who were under
intense persecution, some toying with the idea of returning
to Judaism. He encouraged them not to give up their hope
in Christ or harden their hearts as their ancestors had in the
wilderness. He urged them to help one other avoid slipping
into unbelief and rebellion, not just once but daily.

Living for Christ in an ungodly world is a challenge.
We need each other to stay on track and avoid deception.
"As iron sharpens iron, so a friend sharpens a friend," says
Proverbs 27:17. Let's encourage one another to stand strong
in our faith!

**Oh Lord, help my words to be pleasing to you and
encouraging to others. Whether you lead me to admonish
another to follow you more closely, or receive a similar
message myself, give me the ability to do it with grace.**

GREAT WORK!

"His master replied, 'Well done, good and faithful servant! You have been faithful with a few things; I will put you in charge of many things. Come and share your master's happiness!'"

MATTHEW 25:23 NIV

Well done. Good. Faithful. These are powerful affirmations coming from the master at the conclusion of the parable of the talents. He had given three servants each a different amount of money according to their abilities, entrusting it to their care. Upon his return, he found that two of the servants had doubled his money by investing wisely, which pleased him very much. They were offered promotions and a share in his happiness. The third servant, however, buried his money, unwilling to take the risk of an investment and suffered dire consequences.

What can we learn from this parable? There are probably many levels of interpretation, but surely one is this: God has entrusted us with valuable commodities to use for his kingdom. He has uniquely gifted each of us in varying ways for his purposes. So whether we teach or serve or administrate, we are investing in the lives of others for the glory of God. The return may only be revealed in heaven—but certainly, there will be an abundance!

Lord, I want to be a good and faithful servant. Help me to see the things I'm good at as being your gift to me to advance your kingdom.

VICTORY OVER FEAR

Don't be afraid, for I am with you. Don't be discouraged,
for I am your God. I will strengthen you and help you. I will
hold you up with my victorious right hand.

ISAIAH 41:10 NLT

This is one of the most magnificent promises in the Bible, is it not? In just a few words, it reassures us that no matter how fearful, discouraged, weak, and helpless we are, we need not fear. The almighty God is with us and because of his presence, all is well.

A tiny child will completely fall apart when his mother leaves the room because his security is bound up in her presence. She is his source of security and without her, he is afraid. And so it is with us. As children of God, we must rely on our heavenly Father's presence. Be encouraged! God is with you—upholding you with his victorious right hand.

Father, thank you for this precious promise of your presence. Without you, I can do nothing. I will put my trust in you today and hold on to your hand.

THE COST OF FREEDOM

He is so rich in kindness and grace that he purchased our
freedom with the blood of his Son and forgave our sins.
EPHESIANS 1:7 NLT

We often forget what our freedom means for us. We live in
a society of equal rights, freedom of speech, and a plethora of
personal choice. You don't have to go too far back into history,
however, to realize that this freedom came at a cost.

In the same way, God paid a price for our spiritual
freedom. We may take for granted that all we did to be saved
was repent. When we have sinned, we are able to boldly ask
for forgiveness and walk away from the penalty. While this
is the wonderful freedom of Christian living, sometimes it is
beneficial to remind ourselves that we were once slaves to sin
and destined for death. God's incredible kindness took this
sentence from us. Take a moment to confess your sins before
God and rejoice in your freedom.

Jesus, I ask for your forgiveness. I thank you that your
grace is enough to cover all of my sin. Thank you for your
great sacrifice so I can be free. I choose to walk in this
freedom today.

A GOOD INVESTMENT

Give generously to them and do so without a grudging heart; then because of this the Lord your God will bless you in all your work and in everything you put your hand to.

DEUTERONOMY 15:10 NIV

You simply cannot out-give God. A young couple learned this truth in a very practical way. Wanting to follow the Lord in giving, but literally having nothing to give, they prayed. That very week, they received a special monetary gift from a friend and immediately passed it along. Within a very short time, they had received ten times over the amount they had given!

Certainly, we do not give to get and there are so many ways to give other than monetarily, but the principle remains. When we willingly give of our time, energy, and resources, God has promised to return every investment with interest.

Thank you, Lord, for your generosity to me. As I give to others, may your provision and blessing pour back to me to be invested once again.

NO PLACE FOR PRIDE

He gives more grace. Therefore He says:
"God resists the proud,
But gives grace to the humble."

JAMES 4:6 NKJV

James wrote his letter to Jewish Christians to expose their sinful behavior and give them instructions on how to live correctly. The believers were angry, envious, quarrelling with one another. They were selfish and prideful to the core.

God wastes no affection on pride; he resists it just as the proud resist him. However, his grace flows continually to the humble of heart, to those who are willing to lay down their own way for the sake of others. He bestows more grace to those who know their weaknesses and therefore depend on him.

O Lord, how wonderful it is to know that you give grace and then more grace, enough to meet every need. Help me to turn away from pride and self-sufficiency and receive your grace for another day.

JOYFUL GROWTH

"These things I have spoken to you, that my joy may remain in you, and that your joy may be full."
JOHN 15:11 NKJV

What are "these things" Jesus is referring to? Surely, it is important to know, as they are the source of the joy that can be ours. In the first part of the chapter, Jesus uses a metaphor that explains the meaning. He is the vine, he says. We are the branches. When we remain attached to the life-giving vine, we will bear fruit, and in so doing, glorify the Father. From the security of this oneness comes joy.

Jesus longs for us to experience the joy he has with his Father. Out of abiding comes joy and fruitfulness. As you pour out his love to others today, God will fill you up with his full, complete, and overflowing joy.

Lord, I love this promise of joy that overflows. I know it does not come from any outside source, but from your Spirit directly to mine. I choose today to abide in you and to trust you for joy.

INCREASED INSIGHT

This is my prayer: that your love may abound more and more in knowledge and depth of insight, so that you may be able to discern what is best and may be pure and blameless for the day of Christ.

PHILIPPIANS 1:9-10 NIV

Paul prayed for the Christians in Philippi from his jail cell with love and concern for their spiritual welfare. He prayed with joy and thanksgiving because of the wonderful partnership in the gospel they shared. He wanted their love to grow deeper as they knew Christ better, having increased insight in making wise decisions and remaining pure and blameless until Christ's return.

Isn't this powerful to pray for ourselves and those under our guidance? There is an old saying that "more is caught than taught." Perhaps as we teach, what will be caught will be the love, wisdom, and purity of life they see in us.

Lord, I pray that my love for others would abound more and more. I pray I would learn to know you better and live a pure life that will draw others to you.

MONKEY SEE, MONKEY DO

In all things show yourself to be an example of good deeds, with purity in doctrine, dignified, sound in speech, which is beyond reproach, so that the opponent will be put to shame, having nothing bad to say about us.

TITUS 2:7-8 NASB

A well-known Christian speaker and author sat at a conference table one afternoon with several others. The tantalizing aroma of coffee wafted through the air. As time went on, it was obvious people were getting restless and needed a break, yet no one made a move. Finally, the gentleman pushed back his chair, stood up, and said, "I'm going to get myself a cup of coffee." Immediately, every other person in the room stood to their feet and made a beeline for the coffee. The old adage is true: "Monkey see; monkey do!"

Paul knew the importance of this principle, so he wrote a letter to Titus, his young son in the faith, to instruct him in ministry. Listen to how the New Living Translation puts it: "Be an example to them by doing good works of every kind. Let everything you do reflect the integrity and seriousness of your teaching." Let's be that kind of role model so that we can honestly say with Paul, "You should imitate me, just as I imitate Christ."

Thank you, Lord, for the instructions you so clearly set out for us in your Word. Help me to model Jesus to my students through my words and my actions.

ADD TO THE ENSEMBLE

Let love and faithfulness never leave you;
bind them around your neck,
write them on the tablet of your heart.

PROVERBS 3:3 NIV

Getting ready for the day is a ritual for a woman—the hair, the face, the outfit, the shoes, the accessories. When one element is missing, she feels incomplete. According to Proverbs, she is to add to her ensemble love, mercy, kindness, and truth. She is to bind them securely around her neck like a valuable necklace, so she does not forget.

In Biblical times, Jewish men wore phylacteries (small leather boxes containing Scripture) on their heads or arms as a physical reminder to keep the law. Now, rather than a visible memorandum, we are to write them on the tablets of our hearts—a sort of journal of the soul. Let's be teachers whose hearts are engraved with love and faithfulness, for in doing so, we will find favor with both God and people.

Lord, help me to record your Word in my heart so I will remember your love and faithfulness to me. I want to be inseparable from your truths so they flow naturally through my life to others.

PEACE TREATY

Let the peace of Christ rule in your hearts, since as
members of one body you were called to peace.
And be thankful.

COLOSSIANS 3:15 NIV

The disciples, tossed around in the midst of a terrible storm at sea, were terrified! Jesus, walking on the water, brought peace to the tempest. He is the peace giver. The peace of Christ is more than mere tranquility of the soul. We need to let it have governing authority. When we do, we know all is well. When it eludes us, we know something is amiss.

This is true for the whole body of Christ. We are all called to let peace rule in us individually and corporately and to be filled with thanksgiving to God for this gift which passes understanding. Let your heart be at rest today, trusting in his presence, confident that he will guide, guard, and protect you with his amazing peace.

My heart is so grateful, Lord, for the peace you give me, even in the most trying of circumstances. I chose today to allow your peace to govern my life.

WHEN WORDS FAIL

*The Spirit also helps our weakness; for we do not know
how to pray as we should, but the Spirit Himself intercedes
for us with groanings too deep for words.*

ROMANS 8:26 NASB

Our dependence upon God is absolute and complete.
"Without me you can do nothing," Jesus said. So great is our
weakness that we even need God to pray like we ought. In
Exodus 2, God's people groaned under their burden of slavery
and cried out for help. Their cry rose up to God, who heard and
knew it was time to act. When the need is so intense, sometimes
words do not come. That is the moment the Holy Spirit
intervenes; his intercession rises to the throne on our behalf.

At times we wander much like the Israelites did in the
wilderness, unsure of the direction God wants us to go and
unable to even pray. As God once lead his people with a
pillar of cloud and fire, so he will lead his children today.
Be encouraged. The Spirit of God knows your heart and is
translating your groanings into prayers.

**Oh God, thank you for this precious and magnificent
assurance that in my profound weakness, your Spirit is
interceding for me. I rest in that knowledge today.**

THE TEXTBOOK OF LIFE

All Scripture is breathed out by God and profitable for teaching, for reproof, for correction, and for training in righteousness, that the man of God may be complete, equipped for every good work.

2 TIMOTHY 3:16-17 ESV

If you had been a teacher during the 18th or 19th centuries, your reading textbook would have been the New England Primer. The ABCs were taught by stories from the Bible, which not only taught the children to read, but gave morals for living as well. Sadly, as secularism infiltrated society, laws were written to remove religious education from our schools. Test scores dropped, morals declined, and crime began to rise.

There is no substitute for the Word of God. It is useful to teach us what is true and to make us realize what is wrong in our lives. It corrects us and teaches us to do what is right. God uses it to prepare and equip his people to do every good work. What better textbook could there be than one written by God? You are being trained by it so that you can train others.

Lord, how I love your Word—given directly from your heart to ours. I want to continue to be trained in righteousness so I will be equipped to instruct others.

ACT OF SURRENDER

I trust in you, O Lord;
I say, "You are my God."
My times are in your hand.
PSALM 31:14-15 ESV

There are certain times in our life when we'd like full control. We'd like to believe that if we just put enough work into the issue we are facing, we'd come up with the solution all on our own. This can leave us tired, spinning more and more into frustration as we rely solely on our human flesh to do something God asks us to let him do.

How glorious it is that we serve a God who is in control. He assures us our time is in his hand and we can walk in bold trust, releasing all we've tried so hard to keep together. Letting go is a beautiful act of surrender.

Lord, give me a greater understanding of how to trust you in each situation. I freely surrender my control to you and ask you to take this burden I'm carrying.

UNSEEN MYSTERIES

"Have you believed because you have seen me? Blessed are those who have not seen and yet have believed."
JOHN 20:29 ESV

The early years of childhood are filled with questions about things kids can't see with their eyes. "Teacher, is the Easter Bunny real?" "Do you think Santa put me on the nice list?" Without question, children desire to believe in something they can't see because of the joy it brings them. The mystery, magic, and excitement around certain events and holidays can be enough to stir their hearts into believing in those mysteries with all their might.

What a privilege it is that you have the gifting to lead and instruct children about the Creator of the universe, the mystery they cannot see. What an honor to pray over them, that they may become part of a bigger family of people who trust by faith not by sight.

Remind me, God, of the young hearts I get to work with every day. Give me wisdom in leading them closer to you. Even when they cannot see you, let them trust in you.

SAVIOR

When I am with those who are weak, I share their
weakness, for I want to bring the weak to Christ.
Yes, I try to find common ground with everyone,
doing everything I can to save some.

1 CORINTHIANS 9:22 NLT

To try to save someone is a heroic act. It can feel like an overwhelming task to take on, especially when you are given a lens into another's life and see the reality of what that rescue might look like. Often you need to put yourself in their shoes to grapple for an understanding of what they are truly facing, and this can feel heavy and helpless.

The ultimate salvation came when Jesus died on the cross for each one of us. He walked on earth and knows the weaknesses we struggle with. He shares them, carrying the heavy burden for us. What a comfort it is to know the Savior of the world knows us intimately. We never fight alone.

Jesus, when I see someone who is hurting, guide me in how to minister to them. Whisper to me in the tough conversations. Encourage me in the truth that you see me and you see the person I am fighting for.

IN THE STORM

O love the LORD, all you His godly ones!
The LORD preserves the faithful
and fully recompenses the proud doer.
Be strong and let your heart take courage,
all you who hope in the LORD.

PSALM 31:23-24 NASB

You might currently feel as though you are stuck in a storm of confusion, wallowing in a sea of grief, on the edge of a tidal wave of emotion, or simply having a rough day. These trying times are not easy to navigate, and hopelessness can set in. We weren't meant to tackle this life on our own.

Cling to the truth of the Word in distress. Hold on to the reminder that God will preserve you, give you strength, and breathe hope into your life. Let his words of courage speak to your heart and be the only words you hear.

Father God, when I'm walking through the fire, remind me that courage comes from you. Speak to my heart the truth I already know: you go before me every step of the way.

WORDS OF LIGHT

The entrance of Your words gives light;
It gives understanding to the simple.

PSALM 119:130 NKJV

Every day, as an educator, you stand in front of someone and your words an impact. Whether little ones or older, they sit and listen to what you say. Your words can change their lives: a light bulb turning on a new idea, a word of encouragement that brightens a child's day, a note of praise to a co-worker for a job well done, a positive conference time with worried parents, a voice of reason in a difficult situation.

Words matter. As the words of Jesus breathe light into our lives, let your words do the same for others. Jesus spoke words of love. Be encouraged to be like Christ today, and let your love speak volumes.

Jesus, help me to use my words wisely. Teach me to show love using my words. Help me soak in your Word and give light to my life, so I can pass that light on to others.

GOD WITH YOU

The LORD your God is in your midst,
a mighty one who will save;
he will rejoice over you with gladness;
he will quiet you by his love;
he will exult over you with loud singing.

ZEPHANIAH 3:17 ESV

In busy workdays, in long hours of preparation, in loving difficult kids, in tough conversations, remember who is there. Remember the one who put this desire, this gift of teaching, in your life. He delights in your work, friend, and he rejoices over you.

Days can be long and tiring, but God is with you every step of the way, saving you, rejoicing over you, and quieting you with his love. He is more than enough: more than the throw-up on your shoe, the fight you broke up over recess, the relentless parent you have to talk to... again. When you need to know that he is with you, ask him to reveal himself. He will.

God, thank you that you are a Father who walks with me. Help me to rejoice in your love as you rejoice in me. Despite my circumstance, I want to remember you are the one I serve.

UNIQUELY MADE

O LORD, what a variety of things you have made!
In wisdom you have made them all.
The earth is full of your creatures.

PSALM 104:24 NLT

There is probably nothing more revealing about the creativity and perfect design of God's creatures than looking at a classroom full of his children. Not one of them is alike. They are all like little snowflakes; uniquely created, woven together in a distinct way.

"In wisdom you have made them all." Each one of these children was made for a purpose. In God's astuteness, he created no one person the same. That creativity can certainly make your job tougher as you instruct multiple personalities and learning styles. As you teach, remember who created each child, and know that you are helping mold them into exactly who God has called them to be.

Lord, remind me of my purpose with the children you have entrusted to my care. As I instruct, give me wisdom to see who you have designed them to be. Help me to see each one as you see them.

TEACHER OR PARENT?

Remind them to be subject to rulers and authorities, to be obedient, to be ready for every good work, to speak evil of no one, to avoid quarreling, to be gentle, and to show every courtesy to everyone.

TITUS 3:1-2 NRSV

On certain days, being a teacher means being a temporary parent. You're responsible for ensuring your students make wise choices, use good behavior, get along with their peers, are respectful and courteous, and ultimately obey what you're asking of them. What a huge responsibility!

When we follow the Word of God, he gives us a lot of the tools we need. He doesn't say it will be easier, but he does promise eternal reward when our hearts pursue him first. Ultimately, our desire as believers is to spread the love of Jesus and encourage others in their walk. This means our peers, younger children, spouses, neighbors—those we encounter in our everyday life. As a teacher, you have access to many hearts and minds. Treat them as Jesus would.

God, my job is so many different things. On the harder days when I feel as though I am raising these kids, remind me that they are yours first and that you have asked me to help you be known in their life. Help me to love them as you do.

THE WORRY TRAIN

*"Which of you by worrying can add a single hour
to his life's span?"*

LUKE 12:25 NASB

Stress can be an active participant in the life of a teacher.
If not kept in check, it soon becomes the only participant.
You wake up every day feeling the immediate weight of the
day in front of you. This can lead to unhealthy attitudes and
lifestyle choices, and general unhappiness. Worry and stress
do nothing to your life but give the enemy a chance to bring
you down. Recognizing that stress leads to worry, frustration,
and unhappiness makes you aware that stress needs a release.
Friend, you can do this in Christ!

Jesus brings light and life to a situation that seems endless
and worrisome. He promises to take it from you and replace it
with peace. Peace, amidst a crazy busy job, can be a beautiful
reminder that releasing stress and worry is possible. Peace in
Jesus reminds you of what is important—what truly matters.
Peace gives you hope in the everyday routine.

**Father God, I don't want to spend another minute worrying
about this situation. I release it to you and ask you to take
it. I feel like I'm spinning and I need you to stop it for me.
Take it, Jesus, and replace my worry with peace.**

WORDS

The wise are known for their understanding.
Their pleasant words make them better teachers.
PROVERBS 16:21 NCV

You have a gift, brave teacher, of being patient, wise, and understanding to a variety of people. This is not a role everyone can fill. Today, feel confident in the calling God has placed in your life to teach. It is not a job just anyone can do.

If today is one of those days where you aren't feeling like this is the best role for you, if your words haven't been so pleasant, your heart hasn't been so fulfilled, press into the Lord even more. He will remind you of the gifting he has placed on your heart and the joy you can have when you use it. He will uphold you with his hand and guide your decisions. He will rejoice over you with song and breathe new life into your soul when you need it the most.

God, I don't always feel like using pleasant words and being known for my understanding. Today, remind me why you've called me to this position. Give me your words, filled with grace and love, for those I will encounter this day.

COFFEE BREAK

Examine everything carefully; hold fast to that which is good; abstain from every form of evil.

1 THESSALONIANS 5:21 NASB

Peer pressure never goes away. Whether out on the playground or in the break room, there is always a choice between good and evil. Gossip, slander, intentional harm—all are forms of evil, sin that can rule our daily life. This can be a slippery slope, especially among co-workers. A negative comment one week can turn into a daily bash session.

The Bible tells us to examine *everything*. To sift through your thoughts and actions, hold on to the good, and get rid of the evil. Stand firm against the enemy who delights in deceiving you. Think of the example you can set for co-workers when they notice your silence in the gossip, or see you leave an unkind conversation. They will recognize you are different. That difference is Jesus.

Examining everything can feel like a lot, Jesus. Please give me discernment. I want to move forward knowing I am examining my heart and following your lead. Thank you for guiding me.

RENEWAL

*We do not lose heart, but though our outer man is
decaying, yet our inner man is being renewed day by
day. For momentary, light affliction is producing for us an
eternal weight of glory far beyond all comparison.*

2 Corinthians 4:16-17 nasb

There are many times as a teacher you feel frustrated or
impatient. When a student forgets to put their name on their
paper, again. When that group of kids races down the hallway
for the tenth time. When your noisy class interrupts your
teaching, for the fifteenth time that day. You want to chastise
the students, "How many times do I have to tell you…?" You
want to raise your voice to override the interruption. These
immediate reactions are followed by the gentle reminder that
we serve a God who forgives us time and time again for the
same mistakes.

The Father calls us to the same patient endurance that is
only achievable by his grace. Try to see his children as he does
today. Put a sticky note on your computer that says "renewed
day by day" or "patience" to remind you that God calls you to
forgive and instruct. This simple act will speak volumes to your
students.

**Jesus, thank you for nurturing my spirit daily. I praise
you for the way you tell me I can start new. Thank you for
loving me despite my flaws and giving me your grace.**

THE SEVENTH DAY

By the seventh day God had finished the work he had been doing; so on the seventh day he rested from all his work. Then God blessed the seventh day and made it holy, because on it he rested from all the work of creating that he had done.

GENESIS 2:2-3 NIV

Picture God on the seventh day, looking at everything he had just created and breathing a contented sigh of relief. A day of rest. One day among the crazy-busy six other days. After a long week of work, that day of rest is glorious. Taking time to rest takes effort; it is a delicate balance between checking items off your to-do list and having personal time to reflect and rejuvenate.

Take this day of Sabbath as an invitation from the Lord. A day to say no to unnecessary things and yes to rest. A day to be still—preparing for the week ahead. A day to be with a friend, your family, or just yourself, and breathe a contented sigh of relief. You are doing good work. Take this day of Sabbath as a gift.

God, thank you for giving me a day of rest. Thank you for giving me time to worship you, be still with you, and be refueled to prepare for the week. Give me purpose and direction as I spend quiet time with you.

UNSPEAKABLE

Before the mountains were brought forth,
or ever you had formed the earth and the world,
from everlasting to everlasting you are God.

PSALM 90:2 ESV

There are times when a single act can change your entire perspective. Whether you teach in a public school or not, the school shootings over the past two decades have caused everyone to mourn. If you're an educator in the public school system, you may have had to take extra steps to safeguard yourselves and your students and be prepared for the unthinkable. This hardly seems like something you signed up for when your heart was drawn to teaching.

God reminds us in his Word that he is who he says he is. Everlasting to everlasting, no matter what the enemy does on this earth, God is still God. He is a good God: a God who loves, who mourns when we mourn, who will come again and defeat all evil. There will be no more tears, no more death, and no more sadness. Praise him for that promise!

God, help these promises seep into my soul and settle there. Speak your truth to me in the Word as I prepare for another day.

THE GREAT MYSTERY

Oh, the depth of the riches both of the wisdom and knowledge of God! How unsearchable are His judgments and unfathomable His ways!

ROMANS 11:33 NASB

Teachers need wisdom for certain situations. *What is the appropriate response to this child's question? How do I handle this particular parent? What do I say to my co-worker?* Luckily, we have prayer. Prayer allows us to bring all of these wisdom-seeking situations to the Lord.

God desires a relationship with us—a space where we communicate our hearts and listen for his response. There is so much to be gained from the knowledge of God. He is beyond our human comprehension and sometimes so very mysterious. But in all of the mystery, there is sovereignty and love. When you're seeking wisdom, seek out God.

Father God, thank you for your love. You determine my steps and impart discernment when I need it. Help me to come to you first before trying to solve things on my own.

GIFTS FOR FREE

"Love your enemies, and do good, and lend, expecting nothing in return, and your reward will be great, and you will be sons of the Most High, for he is kind to the ungrateful and the evil."

LUKE 6:35 ESV

Loving those who are difficult to love is probably one of the hardest things to do. It requires selflessness, humility, and compassion. It takes courage too: courage to love as Jesus did, even when we don't feel it is deserved. God asks us to love our enemies, those very people most difficult to love, and expect nothing in return. Give your gifts of love away. Expect nothing back.

God also promises a great reward. As you approach each day knowing you will encounter those who are difficult to love, do so with courage and compassion. Give your love away for free and know your reward in heaven is coming.

Lord, thank you that you showed me how to love. Thank you for your grace when I'm around those who are more difficult to love, those who require more of me. Give me courage and understanding in my conversations and actions.

UNCOMMON

The grace of God has appeared that offers salvation to all people. It teaches us to say "No" to ungodliness and worldly passions, and to live self-controlled, upright and godly lives in this present age.

TITUS 2:11-12 NIV

The age we live in is filled with immediate gratification: a young culture focused on entitlement and millions of dollars spent on unnecessary things. It is easy to get caught up in it and forget our role and purpose as Christians. To live a godly life is to live a life more uncommon: a life with a purpose for others instead of ourselves, a life where we say no to worldly passions.

Your greatest impact can come in choosing this uncommon life. In doing so, people start to wonder why you put others before yourself. It's a great ministering opportunity for those in your life who are curious.

God, help me to choose the unbeaten path in this world of overindulgence. Give me wisdom for how to handle situations and my earthly desires. Help me to live a life where people ask me why.

UNSHAKABLE

Let us be grateful for receiving a kingdom that cannot be shaken, and thus let us offer to God acceptable worship, with reverence and awe.

HEBREWS 12:28 ESV

Remaining in constant communion with the Lord is a gift to your day. Amid the crazy schedules, tough conversations, work lunches, and responsibility, God fills your life with reminders of his love and joy.

Remember, today, that he wins and that his kingdom cannot be shaken. Take time to stand in awe of all he has done and will do in his coming promise of return. It is easy to stand in wonder of his majesty, and he loves to hear your worship, your songs, your praise, and your heart. Let him be part of your day today.

Lord Jesus, may I take time today to worship you, to stand in awe of all you've done and will do. You cannot be shaken, and I am so thankful for that.

AUGUST

Watch yourselves, so that you may
not lose what we have worked for,
but may win a full reward.

2 John 1:8 esv

EVERYDAY ROUTINE

Whether you eat or drink, or whatever you do,
do all to the glory of God.
1 CORINTHIANS 10:31 NKJV

It may seem overwhelming to read this particular verse. It will help to remember that what counts in all the things you do is your heart's posture toward God. Paul isn't saying that while you brush your teeth you need to simultaneously be preaching the good news. He is saying, however, that even in the everyday, mundane things you can bring glory to the one who has made it all possible. He is saying that your heart posture can always be pointing in the direction of your Father.

In a life filled with everyday routine, it is comforting to keep your focus on the source of peace. God is the one who deserves the glory for the life you are living, even in difficulties. Bringing him glory brings you happiness and peace because it keeps God at the forefront of your heart.

God, thank you for the life you've given me. In the everyday mundane details, help me to see you and hear you proclaiming joy and peace over my life.

ABIDE IN HIM

His anointing teaches you about everything, and is true,
and is no lie—just as it has taught you, abide in him.
1 JOHN 2:27 ESV

As believers, we know that Jesus is the source of all life. We read his Word and learn from it. We soak in knowledge from the truth of what he tells us, and we trust. One thing he asks; that we abide in him. As we grow in spiritual maturity this becomes an easier concept to hold onto.

The principle of abiding and remaining can be a great learning opportunity for someone who is newer in the faith or going through a tough situation. It isn't always easy to keep your eyes on the author of peace or to want to remain with him when you feel lost, confused, or broken. As brothers and sisters in Christ, let us encourage one another in the faith and promise of Jesus.

Jesus, thank you that you do not lie. What I read in your Word brings light and life to my soul. May I teach others about your truth and the love that we receive when we abide in you.

CONTENTMENT

*I know what it is to be in need, and I know what it is to
have plenty. I have learned the secret of being content
in any and every situation, whether well fed or hungry,
whether living in plenty or in want.*

PHILIPPIANS 4:12 NIV

Oh how difficult this can be! Contentment in any and every situation? It's something we continually learn in our walk with Jesus. It doesn't matter what we have or don't have; what matters is where our hearts are directed and where we put our trust. Our understanding of contentment grows as we learn that God doesn't change even when our situations do.

Contentment is a skill. It is putting your trust in a God who says he loves you and is always for you. It is a maturity of faith that comes with an abundance of grace. As you grow in this area, your trust deepens. Give yourself grace to grow in understanding of a God who does not change even when your situation does and be encouraged today.

Jesus, thank you that you are unchanging. My situation sometimes feels like a daily battle, but you are always walking with me. Help me as I learn to trust you, knowing that you walk before me.

LIFTER OF YOUR HEAD

You, O LORD, are a shield about me,
my glory, and the lifter of my head.

PSALM 3:3 ESV

Today, be reminded that God is your comforter. He does not leave you. He knows whatever is before you, and he protects you as a shield protects a warrior. He lifts your head when you want to put it down. He tells you to look up and see his smile shining down on you. He is proud of you, and his love will never fail.

Whatever is before you today, know who is walking beside you holding your hand. As you step out in faith, know who is lighting your path. As you cry, know who lifts your head. What a good Father he is!

God, thank you for protecting me, for sending your Son to die for me so I can be free. Thank you for always walking with me and seeing me as I am.

AT THE CROSS

I waited patiently for the Lord;
and He inclined to me, and heard my cry.

PSALM 40:1 NKJV

There might be something staring you in the face right now that God is imploring you to lay at his feet. A situation weighing you down, a student you can't reach, a dysfunctional relationship, a stressful job situation; God wants it all. He wants you to let it go. He sent his Son so you could be free from carrying the things that weigh you down.

What a loving Father we serve. His Son carried the heaviest cross of all for us. God might not always respond the way we would like, or as quickly as we would like, but we can lay our burdens down anyway, knowing that he hears us and will carry them for us.

Jesus, thank you for dying for me. Thank you for carrying the cross for my sin and my pain. You are so loving and gracious, and I praise you!

PEACE OFFERING

All your children will be taught by the LORD,
and great will be their peace.

ISAIAH 54:13 NIV

As a teacher and follower of Jesus, the Lord has given you a gift—a gift of teaching in his name, a promise of peace with instruction from God. What a beautiful picture for approaching each day of teaching. What a joy! As you open the Word of God, he fills you up with peace that surpasses all understanding.

Today, before you begin your routine, make Jesus and his Word a priority. Let his truth speak life into your soul and give you peace, so you can go and make his peace known. As you teach his children, may his words be your words; let his peace flow freely from your lips.

Jesus, thank you that you are the giver of peace! No matter what I face today, you are here. Give me perspective as I seek you, and may your words be mine.

STUDENT OF THE LIVING GOD

If you receive my words,
and treasure my commands within you,
so that you incline your ear to wisdom,
and apply your heart to understanding...
then you will understand the fear of the LORD,
and find the knowledge of God.

PROVERBS 2:1-2, 5 NKJV

As a teacher you understand that knowledge is gained from studying. Applying yourself to a particular subject gives you greater depth to that area of interest. The Word of God is similar. Walking with God requires studying his Word, taking the truth of what he says and letting it all soak in. These words become treasures you rely on. The knowledge of God is deep and his Word has great power to change your life. But it takes carving out time to read, study, and retain.

Becoming a master student of the Word of God doesn't just happen. The more you dive in, the more in love with him you become. Your ear will seek out his wisdom. The more you understand, the more you will find knowledge of who he says he is, and he never lets you down. You fall more deeply in love and your life is transformed!

God, let me make time for your Word today. Let me do as I tell my students to do and apply myself so I can get to know you more. May your words penetrate my soul and make me fall more in love with who you are.

A REFUGE FROM THE STORM

The LORD also will be a refuge for the oppressed,
A refuge in times of trouble.
Those who love Your name will put their trust in You;
for You, LORD, have not forsaken those who seek You.
PSALM 9:9-10 NKJV

When you teach, you give your students tactics to be prepared. For example, when you are given fair warning that a storm is approaching, you encourage them to protect themselves. You instruct them to find supplies, shelter, and light for the darkness. But how do you prepare your students when they are given no warning? What do you encourage them to cling to in the darkness?

Jesus says he is the light. He is your refuge in time of trouble. Putting your trust in him means you will never be forsaken. When you find yourself in the middle of a storm, call out his name, and you will know he is there. In the darkness of shadows, his light will appear. This instruction is the greatest gift you can give your students—they will know who to cling to during the unexpected storms of life.

God, help me to bring your light to my students today. Give me wisdom with how to instruct them in love and preparedness for your coming return.

BEFORE WE ASK

Your lovingkindness, O Lord, extends to the heavens,
Your faithfulness reaches to the skies.

PSALM 36:5 NASB

When you feel you cannot love, God says he can. When you are weak, he is strong. When you can't choose good, God says he is good. If you are in that place today, remember God is faithful. He extends beyond our understanding and knows what we need before we ask.

Rest in that promise today. Whatever is on your heart you can put at his feet and he will take care of it. In his faithfulness, he asks that we are faithful back—trusting him. We trust that he is loving and good and just, all in one. Nothing gets past him without him knowing and he sees us when we don't feel seen. He adores his children!

God, thank you for your faithfulness in always loving me when I don't feel I deserve it. Thank you for forgiving me and seeing me despite my flaws. Let me hear your sweet whispers of love today.

TEACHING HATS

We are God's workmanship, created in Christ Jesus to do good works, which God prepared in advance for us to do.
EPHESIANS 2:10 NIV

As a teacher, you wear many hats. You nurse kids that are hurt, or send them home if they have a fever. You mentor students who are lost in a subject, or give them guidance in certain areas of their life. You become a coach, encouraging each individual in his or her daily walk. You are an instructor, guiding and teaching knowledge with varying learning styles.

Remember that you were given these gifts and Jesus walks with you as you balance all your roles. When you are struggling with a particular hat, lean on him. Ask him to lead you, and he will. You were created to do his good works and you are a blessing to others in so many ways, every day!

God, thank you for giving me the gift of teaching. As I juggle my hats, please fill me up where I need it most. I love to serve you through this gift and I thank you for giving it to me.

FAITH IN LOVE

*The important thing is faith—the kind of faith
that works through love.*

GALATIANS 5:6 NCV

Many of your students or colleagues might need a dose of faith: of believing in something higher than themselves. They need someone to tell them they are treasured, and they are seen. Hopelessness is a reality in the world today and it comes in varying forms.

God says love is the framework for faith. In your role as a teacher, you can spread love in a beautiful way: a love that paves the way for faith, a love that speaks volumes to the Jesus you serve, a love that is inconceivable to the one draped in hopelessness. As you seek God's love in a greater way, he will give you more to spread. Everyone has struggles. Remember this as you interact each day, and show faith in love.

Father, remind me that all of your children are meant to be loved. Give me an endless amount of love to lavish on others.

STORY TELLING

Seek to do good to one another and to everyone.
1 THESSALONIANS 5:15 ESV

In your profession, you probably encounter a lot of stories. You will hear from students, parents, and co-workers from varying walks of life, each with their story to tell. Sometimes those stories preclude us from seeing the person as Jesus would. Often, we make judgments and reach our own conclusions first.

Jesus had disciples of the sorriest kind—people who sinned and questioned and doubted. However, they chose to follow Jesus when others wouldn't. They chose to step out on the water and trust that he would keep them afloat. That kind of faith doesn't come on our own accord. That comes when we ask for wisdom and discernment. When we encounter those who are hard to love, or whose stories seem to hold too much weight, we should remember who is beside us ready to help.

If I encounter someone today that is tougher for me to love, Jesus, remind me that they are your child just as I am. Give me love and understanding where I find it hard to summon up.

LET IT GO!

In your anger do not sin: Do not let the sun go down while you are still angry, and do not give the devil a foothold.
EPHESIANS 4:26 NIV

Students can be very challenging at times. At the end of a long day, it can be easy to let the irritation get the best of you. Jesus never condemned feelings of anger, only the sin that often follows. When anger is not diffused, it can lead to saying or doing the wrong thing.

God gives us a strategy to deal with our anger, and that is to deal with it quickly—not carry it with us for the rest of the day. God understands our frustrations. The next time you feel yourself reacting, send a prayer his way and ask him to deal with the feelings. Instead of giving the devil an advantage, give it to the Lord and let him win the battle for you.

Lord, I am sorry when I have allowed anger to reside in my heart for too long. I give my frustration with particular people and situations to you. Thank you for the grace you give me to face difficult things.

FIRM FAITH

For God so loved the world that he gave his one and only Son, that whoever believes in him shall not perish but have eternal life. For God did not send his Son into the world to condemn the world, but to save the world through him. Whoever believes in him is not condemned.

JOHN 3:16, 18 NIV

There is a lot of joy in reminding yourself that you are free from the guilt and punishment of wrongdoing. This is the very reason that Jesus was sent into the world. At the heart of the Christian faith lies our belief in Jesus Christ and his power to save us from sin and death. Eternity is our destiny.

As a teacher, there are things that constantly challenge our faith and we can sometimes lose the power of what we believe when we don't center our thoughts on Jesus. Just as you may ask your students to commit important things to memory, you probably have this verse memorized. Take some time today to dwell on what it really means for you.

Thank you, God, for sending your Son into the world so that I can receive eternal life. Thank you that my belief in Jesus means that I am not condemned. Help me share my belief with others so they may be saved through you.

LAND OF PLENTY

Some people are like land that gets plenty of rain. The land produces a good crop for those who work it, and it receives God's blessings.

HEBREWS 6:7 NCV

Do you sometimes wonder if all of the hard work that you put into planning, executing, and evaluating your lessons is actually worth the effort? It doesn't always feel like it, does it? We can walk away from a lesson feeling like it didn't go to plan, or that nothing was really learned.

In this verse, God associates diligence with land that produces something useful and good for those who yield its crops. The focus in this illustration isn't on the content, but rather on the hard work that is put in to preparing it. Students are often rewarded for their effort not just their achievement. God is the same way. Allow him to bless you for your effort, and be encouraged that your students are benefiting from it.

Father God, I lay aside the discouragement that I sometimes allow to take over my thoughts. I thank you that you have given me a job that will produce good things. Help me to remember that you have not forgotten my hard work.

LOVE IN ACTION

If anyone has material possessions and sees a brother or sister in need but has no pity on them, how can the love of God be in that person? Dear children, let us not love with words or speech but with actions and in truth.

1 JOHN 3:17-18 NIV

A Sunday school teacher, before her first day of teaching, was relaying her nervousness to the pastor's wife. "It doesn't matter what you say; it's how you make those children feel." The pastor's wife responded. That was most certainly meant to reassure the teacher, but she felt a little offended instead. She had put a great deal of time and effort into planning what she was going to say.

It is worth considering this advice in light of the verse that affirms love through *action*. We might say that we care about those in need, but have we done anything substantial to help them? God has blessed you in some way—be it a clever mind, an understanding heart, or a steady income. Will you allow God to demonstrate his love through your actions today?

Lord, you know that I feel like I already give of myself day after day, but I thank you for challenging me to continue to show love to those in need. Make me aware of the needs around me, and give me your heart of compassion as you lead me in how to demonstrate love.

TRANSFORMATION

*Behold, I tell you a mystery: We shall not all sleep,
but we shall all be changed.*

1 Corinthians 15:51 NKJV

The early church faced some difficult questions of life and death in light of Jesus' resurrection. When Jesus was raised from the dead, believers could have hope for life after death. Exactly what this looks like is still open for debate. How different will our physical bodies be? Will we have the same personality? Paul doesn't answer these questions in this Scripture, but he does affirm that we will all be changed.

For some of us this is exciting; for others, it is a little intimidating. Life after death is a mystery. As a teacher, it may be hard for you to confront something that cannot be explained; you are wired to know the answers! Be encouraged today that despite our lack of understanding, Jesus gave us hope for our future and this future is *good*.

God, I cannot explain many of your ways; they remain a mystery to me. Thank you that I do not need to know exactly what you have in store for my eternity, although I am convinced that I will be beautifully changed. I choose to live in faith and hope for the future.

RIGHT DIRECTIONS

Direct your children onto the right path,
and when they are older, they will not leave it.
PROVERBS 22:6 NLT

Is there something you have always wanted to learn but just haven't had the time to figure out yet? Maybe it's painting, or music, or a sport. Imagine if you showed up at a class only to be told that you had to figure it out on your own. As you well know, skills need to be taught and then practiced.

Younger children are very dependent, and it can be exhausting to be the one that is depended on—especially if you have a house or classroom full of children! It can be helpful to be reminded that children can't be expected to know what the right path is; they need your direction. Our heavenly Father is the best teacher of all, and he will guide you as you guide those under your care.

Dear Lord, at times I get very weary of constantly telling kids the right thing to do. In these times, remind me that I am teaching life-long skills; remind me of the bigger picture. Give me the grace to teach with kindness and mercy, as you have shown to me.

CHERISHED CHILDREN

Children are a gift from the LORD;
they are a reward from him.
PSALM 127:3 NLT

Have you ever tried on a pair of really good sunglasses that filter the light in such a way that everything you look at seems to be more clear and colorful—they generally make the world look like a brighter place. The way we see things around us can change our attitude especially if we make the effort to put on the right filter.

The Bible tells us very clearly how to view children—as a gift and a reward. Children are to be highly valued and thought of as extremely special. They are given by God, loved by God, and it is with this bright and beautiful filter that we need to view the children in our care. Could you find a little extra grace today for the children in your life as you view them as God's treasures?

Lord, I am thankful for the children that you have placed in my life. These children are a gift from you, and I want to love them in a way that shows them they are cherished by you and valued by society. Give me grace to show them how special they are.

THE CROSS AND BEYOND

"If any of you wants to be my follower, you must turn from your selfish ways, take up your cross daily, and follow me."

LUKE 9:23 NLT

The picture of a bruised and battered Jesus being forced to carry an incredibly heavy cross through dusty roads is probably one you have seen or read about many times. Realizing the suffering of Jesus fills us with sadness, but also with incredible gratefulness, knowing that Jesus' whole life up to the cross and beyond was committed to bringing us redemption.

What do you picture when you are asked to take up your cross? Do you see it as a one-time event? Perhaps, as a teacher, you feel like you wear hardship on a daily basis. Following Jesus comes at a cost, but it is so much more. The cross of Christ also led to freedom from sin and death and power over evil. As you follow Jesus today, remember that while you may be suffering, your commitment is also leading you to the path of victory!

Thank you, Jesus, that you are the ultimate example of sacrifice and that you died for me so I would be redeemed. Give me the strength each day to put aside my selfish desires so I can follow you in victory.

HEAVENLY EXPECTATIONS

*Let us then approach God's throne of grace with
confidence, so that we may receive mercy and find grace
to help us in our time of need.*

HEBREWS 4:16 NIV

When we visit a doctor for an ailment, we expect to receive
something that will improve our condition. When we call up
the plumber, we are pretty sure he's going to be able to fix
our leak. When we finally book that hair appointment, we are
hopeful that we are going to come out of the salon looking
our best.

What expectations do you have of our heavenly king?
Many of us feel unworthy to approach God and ask him to
help us. The Scriptures, however, remind us that God is full of
grace and that we can expect him to show us favor when we
approach him. We can expect that our king will help us in our
time of need. What needs do you have today? Whether small
or big, be bold and approach him with an expectation that he
will be merciful to you.

**Heavenly Father, I thank you that you want me to bring my
needs to you. I thank you that you will be merciful to me,
so I approach you with boldness and expectation that you
will help me.**

UNIQUELY UNITED

I appeal to you, brothers and sisters, in the name of our Lord Jesus Christ, that all of you agree with one another in what you say and that there be no divisions among you, but that you be perfectly united in mind and thought.

1 CORINTHIANS 1:10 NIV

To use the apostle Paul's analogy, the human body is a magnificent example of unity with others. The body is made up of so many different parts and systems, and yet they all try to function together for the same purpose. Everyday activities like walking, eating, and talking require the body to work together.

Do you read this Scripture and feel exasperated at the thought of trying to agree with everyone's opinion? True unity is in realizing that each part of the body is as equally unique as it is essential. This is how we should view our day-to-day interactions with others. Isn't it refreshing to know that God isn't asking us to be, or even think, exactly the same as other people? All we need is to apply our uniqueness to a common goal.

Lord, I have often been frustrated with other people and admit that sometimes I cause divisions. Give me the strength of heart to consider everyone as uniquely needed in this team that you have placed me in. Help me to be united with others for the same purpose.

HUMBLE OPINIONS

Be of the same mind toward one another. Do not set your mind on high things, but associate with the humble. Do not be wise in your own opinion.

ROMANS 12:16 NKJV

Teachers usually have a specialty, and after a number of years will often be considered experts in their field. If you are on this path, you may begin to assume that everyone should know certain things that are basic to your subject. It may be good to remind yourself of the teacher or older sibling that made you feel stupid because you didn't know what they thought you should know.

Scripture warns us not to get too proud with our own wisdom. We know that while being an expert may be admired, it will not be passed on without teaching at the right level. Associate with the humble; guide them from the bottom up. That's what Jesus does for us.

Dear Lord, forgive me if I have been proud with my knowledge. Thank you for giving me a good mind for understanding things. Help me to be able to pass on what I have learned in a humble manner that will cause others to grow.

SEASONED SPEECH

Let your speech always be with grace, as though seasoned
with salt, so that you will know how you should respond to
each person.

COLOSSIANS 4:6 NASB

Communication is an art employed by all teachers. Most
would agree that *what* you communicate is not as important
as *how* you communicate it. A bland meal is still a meal, but
a seasoned meal is far more memorable. Whether we are
teaching a class full of children, or a church congregation, or a
young musician, our words can make an impact.

The Bible instructs us to use grace as our guide when we
are speaking. What does a gracious word look like to you?
Do you recognize gentleness, humility, and encouragement
in your words to others? Take heart; when you show grace in
your communication, God will give you the words that you
need for every situation.

God, you are the author of grace. Allow me to let your
grace filter through my heart and into my words to others.
Let those that I teach hear, understand, and grow because
they have been communicated to in love.

BRILLIANCE FROM ABOVE

The heavens are telling of the glory of God;
And their expanse is declaring the work of His hands.

PSALM 19:1 NASB

An expert science teacher once said that the theory of evolution is the biggest assault on the ingenious imagination of God. This is because macroevolution reduces the brilliance of creation to a self-induced product of time. Whatever your beliefs may be about this scientific theory, one thing is clear in the Scriptures: that God's glory is revealed in creation.

It only takes one look at the expansive sky to know that life is bigger than what we experience on earth. Even a limited understanding of the solar system can leave us awestruck, as can a brilliant display of stars on a clear night. The work of God's hands is awesome, partially known and not fully understood. Does this sound like the God that you experience? Allow yourself to dwell on his creativity today, and be encouraged that this same God created you.

Heavenly Father, I thank you for making yourself known through your creation. Help me to notice your creation today, from the small right through to the expanse of the heavens. Thank you that your ingenuity is something that I can experience; give me an extra touch of your creativity today!

DON'T SIT ON IT!

Do not neglect your gift.... Be diligent in these matters;
give yourself wholly to them, so that everyone may see
your progress.

1 TIMOTHY 4:14-15 NIV

Imagine bringing a gift to a birthday party and then seeing the recipient dump your present to the side and turn their attention elsewhere. Perhaps you have experienced this and wondered what the point in giving the gift was? Most of us know the parable of the man who received talents and then buried them so that they wouldn't be taken. Jesus didn't praise this kind of behavior, and Paul repeats this sentiment in Timothy. We need to use the gifts we've been given.

What is your gift? Have you been diligent in using it for the benefit of others? God doesn't ask for performance, results, or excellence, he asks for diligence. The best witness you can be to those watching you is to use your gift to the best of your ability. That gift was made to bless others!

Father, thank you for blessing me with a gift. Help me to be diligent and to give myself fully to the task at hand so that this calling may impact others. I choose to be thankful rather than resentful of what you have set before me.

WORKING SATISFACTION

To enjoy your work and to accept your lot in life—
that is indeed a gift from God. The person who does
that will not need to look back with sorrow on his past,
for God gives him joy.

ECCLESIASTES 5:20 TLB

It would be fair to say that most people look forward to the weekend rather than the working week. We seem to be wired to detest work; this was part of the curse after all, wasn't it? Is it possible, however, for us to view work as a gift?

Whatever God has given you to do, be it a teacher in a classroom, mission field, church, or at home, he has given because you have a gift that is to be used for others. If you are able to accept this, then be encouraged that you can find joy in knowing that you are doing part of what God created you to do. This can bring incredible satisfaction to your understanding of your "lot in life." Will you allow him to bring you enjoyment through your work today?

Lord Jesus, I want to thank you for giving me a job to teach others. I pray you would help me use this gift with diligence and acceptance, so I can find true joy in doing what you have created me to do.

THE HEART OF THE MATTER

What does it matter? The important thing is that in every way, whether from false motives or true, Christ is preached. And because of this I rejoice. Yes, and I will continue to rejoice.

PHILIPPIANS 1:18 NIV

A little girl asks her mother, "Mommy, what does donzerly mean?" The mother responds that she doesn't know and asks her child where she heard the word. The girl begins to sing the national anthem in a loud voice, "O say can you see, by the donzerly light..."

Sometimes we don't learn things the right way, and sometimes that doesn't matter. In Paul's day, the church was experiencing people who were telling others about Christ, and it wasn't exactly right. Paul chose to rejoice in the fact that the name of Christ was being spread, rather than worrying about the precise theology. Perhaps you don't get across the perfect message today; be encouraged to stay enthusiastic about the higher truth that you are communicating. Sometimes you need to give yourself the grace to say, "What does it matter? God is still on the throne!"

Lord, I don't always get it right, and I thank you for reminding me that you care about the heart of my message. Whether I am teaching something that is directly about you or not, I want your name to be honored.

FAITH NEEDS A VOICE

Faith comes by hearing, and hearing by the word of God.
ROMANS 10:17 NKJV

We have heard how important it is to set aside time to read your Bible, but what if reading wasn't a viable option? This is the challenge that the believers in the ancient church faced where literacy was very uncommon, except for the educated elite. Most believers in the first century only heard Scripture by attending public readings. It would have been important, then, to listen well and commit important truths to memory.

Although most of our Western culture is literate, our challenge is competing with the plethora of options of what to read and what to listen to. As it may have been in the early church, hearing the Word of God requires an intentional act on our part to engage in what the Scripture is saying. It is only when we choose to listen that our faith can grow.

Father God, you have given me many ways to hear your Word. Help me to be committed to seeking time to understand the Scriptures. Increase my faith as I listen to your voice, and allow me to be a voice for those who are seeking truth.

RIGHTEOUS RICHES

With me are riches and honor, enduring wealth and prosperity.
My fruit is better than fine gold; what I yield surpasses choice silver.
I walk in the way of righteousness, along the paths of justice,
bestowing a rich inheritance on those who love me and
making their treasuries full.

PROVERBS 8:18-21 NIV

The lifestyle of the rich and famous has always been one of the most sought after. There is simply something in our human nature that draws us toward being the best, or having the most. It is said that teaching is considered one of the most respected occupations, and yet it's one of the most underpaid. It's unlikely that as a teacher you will experience the kind of wealth that leaves you dripping with gold!

Fortunately, enduring wealth has nothing to do with your occupation and everything to do with your pursuit of wisdom. Proverbs repeatedly compares wisdom and understanding to precious metals and stones. This is because the value of wisdom goes well beyond material things. Prioritizing wise ways will result in rich relationships, prosperous decisions, and flourishing attitudes toward life. Let yourself soak in the "gold" of God's wisdom today.

Lord, I admit that sometimes I complain about the lack of compensation I get for a very challenging occupation! Sometimes I wonder if a different path would have accumulated more wealth for me. I submit these thoughts to you, acknowledging that you have provided well for me. Guide my every decision so that your wisdom will bring me the riches that are better than gold.

255

NO-GRUDGE GIVING

Let each one give as he purposes in his heart, not grudgingly or of necessity; for God loves a cheerful giver.

2 CORINTHIANS 9:7 NKJV

Have you ever taken the long route to the supermarket entrance because a charity collector is sitting outside asking for a donation? It can be a challenge to know when to give and when it's okay not to. God's Word doesn't force us into saying yes to everything, but it does encourage us to look at our hearts on the matter.

Giving comes in all forms, and it is not just financial. You probably give a lot of yourself each day in time, effort, and support. God uses his followers to attend to the needs of others. When you decide in your heart that you are going to give, the Bible instructs you to be cheerful about it. Can you determine in your heart to gladly give of yourself today?

Lord, I thank you for the people you have placed in my life that have happily given to me. Thank you that you give me many good things each day. Open my eyes to the needs around me, and open my heart to giving in wisdom and gladness.

SEPTEMBER

For the word
of the LORD is upright,
and all his work is done
in faithfulness.

PSALM 33:4 ESV

GUIDANCE

We do not enjoy being disciplined. It is painful at the time, but later, after we have learned from it, we have peace, because we start living in the right way.
HEBREWS 12:11 NCV

You probably don't remember learning to write; it is one of those things that seems very natural as an adult. If you are an elementary school teacher, you will know how children in their first year have difficulty grasping a pencil and forming letters. Then comes the painstaking repetition of letters until they are well formed. The whole process requires guidance from a teacher and diligence from the child.

Discipline is more than correction from wrongdoing. Discipline is a way of training: mind, body, and spirit. Perhaps you have put yourself through boot camp, or signed up to a weekly language class, or committed yourself to a daily reading of Scripture. If you have children under your care, you probably recognize discipline as a constant reminder of rights and wrongs, incentives and consequences. It's hard work to get things right, but once you do, it becomes much more natural. If you need to be the disciplinarian today, be encouraged that God uses discipline for personal benefit. Discipline brings peace!

Thank you, Father, that you love me enough to discipline me. Thank you that you have placed people in my life that have guided me through the years. Help me to be a positive guide to my students and to encourage them into a path of right living.

THE GREAT ARCHITECT

We can make our plans,
but the LORD determines our steps.

PROVERBS 16:9 NLT

Ask anyone who has project-planned their dream house
and they will tell you that the key to building the best design
rests in the hands of the architect. One may have grand
ideas of what they want and may even be able to draw the
pictures, but ultimately it is the architect that determines the
dimensions, materials, and construction.

Our God is that great architect and he knows each step
that we need to take in order to build our lives into something
beautiful. As this Scripture says, we can make our plans, and
indeed we do, but we need to place those plans into the hand
of the designer and ask him how to proceed. Are there plans
that you have made recently that need to be given over to the
great architect of life? Trust that he has your best in mind, and
let him determine your next step.

**Lord Jesus, I commit my plans to you. I have many
things that I hope to achieve in the years to come, and
yet I acknowledge that I cannot do anything without your
guidance. Give me wisdom and clarity to hear your voice
in all that I do.**

LOVE TRUTH

Speaking the truth in love, we will grow to become in every respect the mature body of him who is the head, that is, Christ.
EPHESIANS 4:15 NIV

Teenagers are awkward for a number of reasons, but one of those is that they are desperately trying to impress others while struggling to accept themselves for who they are. In their immaturity, teenagers will often avoid the truth, thinking this might protect their image.

As adults, we have learned to be a little more real. We know our strengths and weaknesses and can even laugh at our flaws. In our maturity, we understand that honesty really is the best policy. The Bible reminds us that truth and love lead to maturity because this is who Jesus is. You may be challenged regularly to avoid the truth with students, parents, or other colleagues. Sometimes covering up is the easier option, but it will not cause you to grow. The next time you are faced with speaking the truth, let the love of Christ be reflected in your honesty.

Jesus, you say that you are the truth. I want to follow you as a person of truth. Teach me to be honest in those situations where I would prefer not to be. Show me how to speak the truth in love.

THE RULEBOOK

The whole Bible was given to us by inspiration from God and is useful to teach us what is true and to make us realize what is wrong in our lives; it straightens us out and helps us do what is right.

2 TIMOTHY 3:16 TLB

Most schools have some kind of written regulations to guide the conduct of both teachers and students. There are expectations of attendance, dress, and overall behavior toward others. Rules are useful because they encourage respect for oneself and for others. Do you remember the first time you broke a school rule and how you felt about it?

We know that the Bible is not a book of rules, as some might like to suggest. There is incredible wisdom, encouragement, and freedom to be found in reading this living Word; they are words under God's inspiration! At the same time, this wise book gives us a way to conduct our Christian lives. It leads us to truth, it leads us to repentance, it leads us to righteousness. Take some time today to consider God's "rules" and allow them to straighten you out!

Father, I thank you that you have given me freedom. Thank you that I have a choice to obey your words. Thank you for giving me access to the Scriptures so that I can find out how to do things the right way. Give me the grace that I need today to follow you on the path of righteousness.

A SAFER PATH

People with integrity walk safely,
but those who follow crooked paths will slip and fall.
PROVERBS 10:9 NLT

If you have ever been on a walk through a forest, hike up a mountain, or trek through dense bush, you will know that there are guideposts placed at regular intervals to show that you are on the right path. This path has been marked by experience, showing others the safest route. Ignore the guideposts, and you are likely to get into serious trouble. You may even slip and fall.

It is unfortunate that teachers witness cheating on a regular basis. From an early age, people want to win. Nobody likes to be at the bottom of the class, feel unpopular, or lose a game. Integrity is like those guideposts—it is a marker to keep us all on the right track. Take some time today to remind yourself and perhaps even your students that doing the right thing, especially when no one is watching, is the road to success.

God, help me to be a leader of integrity in this place. Give me the strength to put the stake in the ground when the truth needs to be upheld. Let my integrity be a witness of my faith in you. Keep my feet from falling.

NATURE'S VOICE

You will go out with joy and be led out in peace.
The mountains and hills will burst into song before you,
and all the trees in the fields will clap their hands.

ISAIAH 55:12 NCV

It sounds like a scene from "The Lord of the Rings," with animated trees and speaking mountains. Throughout Scripture, authors use allegory to speak of the necessity of creation to communicate its pain and joy. Nature has its own movement and voice in expressing God's magnificence. Consider the roar of the ocean waves, the whisper of the wind, the waving of branches, the running river.

As God's special creation, we were given a voice to articulate our emotions. He has given us much to be joyful about, despite our weariness and discouragement throughout the week. It is good to remind your soul of the goodness and peace of God and to let this dwell in your heart until you can burst into song and clap your hands with joy. Will you allow God to lead you out of whatever hardship you are facing today?

Thank you, Lord, for your marvelous creation and all that it can teach me about praising you. I thank you that a simple song or clapping of the hands can express the joy and peace I have found in you. Continue to lead me into your goodness.

CHANGED BY KINDNESS

Do you presume on the riches of his kindness and forbearance and patience, not knowing that God's kindness is meant to lead you to repentance?

ROMANS 2:4 ESV

At the end of a school year, teachers will often receive gifts from their students, or parents, as a thank you for the effort put into teaching them for that year. Regardless of whether a student has done well academically, it is heartening to be appreciated for the time you have invested and the patience you have practiced!

There is a time, however, where you hope that your students go beyond being impacted by your kindness to applying your teaching to their studies, and succeeding as a result. This must be how God feels with us at times when we thank him again and again for his kindness and patience with us, and yet we fail to see that he is hoping for change. His love for us is rich and extended to us unconditionally, that we might be compelled to learn, grow, and succeed. Will you allow his kindness to change you today?

Lord, I am sorry if I have taken your kindness for granted. I know that you have been patient with me, and I want to allow your love to change me into a person that can reflect your kindness.

WISE ENTHUSIASM

Enthusiasm without knowledge is no good;
haste makes mistakes.

PROVERBS 19:2 NLT

You might love cake, but without a recipe, you can't bake it. The water can allure you, but without knowing how to swim, you'll go under. You can look forward to a successful career, but without understanding business, you'll probably stay at the bottom rung! God wants you to enjoy life, but one of his wise principles is that you acquire some knowledge before you dive head first into another great idea.

Teachers often remind their students to plan, ask questions, check, and re-check their work. A student may be keen to get the science experiment underway, but without reading the instructions or following the guidelines, they could end up seeing no reaction or blowing something up! We tell people to be careful because we know that things can get done the right way when we take our time. Have you considered gaining some good understanding of a situation before you try to act on it? Be wise with your enthusiasm and guide others to do the same.

Jesus, there are a lot of things right now that I feel like I am rushing through. Give me the wisdom to slow down and be careful with the deeds that you have placed before me, so I don't make mistakes.

COUNSEL OF MANY

Without wise leadership, a nation falls;
there is safety in having many advisers.
PROVERBS 11:14 NLT

The general principle of any governing body—be it a national government, city council, church board, or school parent-teacher association—is that there are always enough people to try to represent the majority of the population they are governing. Without getting into the politics or looking at the pitfalls of government, we know instinctively that there is a certain safety in numbers. History will give us far too many examples of leadership gone wrong—often lying in too much power being given to one person. Indeed, nations have fallen with the wrong person in charge.

When you are given big decisions to make in your home, career, or church, do you seek out counsel from a number of wise people in your life? We are used to doing things without help, so we assume we don't need other people's opinions or advice. Be encouraged that when God places you in a position of leadership, he brings others around you to help you lead. Ask God today who these people are, and then be committed to allowing God to use them in your challenging moments.

Father, thank you for trusting me to lead others. Help me to be a wise leader and rely on the counselors that you have placed in my life. Give me humility to ask for help when I need it.

MODELED BEHAVIOR

*Whatever you have learned or received or heard from me,
or seen in me—put it into practice. And the God of peace
will be with you.*

PHILIPPIANS 4:9 NIV

When you hear the expression "the apple doesn't fall far
from the tree," you remember just how much children end up
becoming like their parents. If your parents have been very
involved in your life, you are probably more like them than
you sometimes would like to admit! The simple truth is that
humans, particularly young people, are heavily influenced by
those who are teaching them.

It can be a little disconcerting to acknowledge that what you
do and say in front of your students can have an impact on their
behavior. Be encouraged that when you follow after God's heart,
you will instinctively model a Christ-like attitude. Encourage your
students to put into practice all of the good things they have
received from the people God has placed in their lives.

**God, I want to please you in everything I do and say. Let
me be aware that others are watching, but please also
remind me that you are gracious and able to cover up for
me when I don't get it right. Thank you for your peace.**

EXPERIENCE OVER KNOWLEDGE

"The student is not above the teacher, but everyone who is fully trained will be like their teacher."
LUKE 6:40 NIV

There are moments in teaching where you realize that your student just might be more intelligent than you are. Somehow they ask the questions that you are currently grappling with, and they seem to be able to stump you; they consistently have you on your toes. This can leave you feeling embarrassed or questioning whether you are fit to teach.

The Scriptures make it pretty clear that the student is not above the teacher. To be fully trained is almost entirely different than being full of intelligence. A student is still a student because they have not had the experience a teacher has had. A student might expect a certain result from an experiment because that is what the book says, but a teacher will know that sometimes other variables cause the experiment to fail. A student may run extremely fast, but a teacher knows it is necessary to pace yourself if you want to win a race. The next time you are feeling particularly challenged, remember that what you give is experience. This can be more valuable than knowledge.

Dear Lord, there are certain students that really push me to my limits. Thank you for these students. Thank you for giving them brilliant minds. Give me the wisdom to know how to teach them with both knowledge and experience.

NIP IT IN THE BUD

Discipline your children, and they will give you peace;
they will bring you the delights you desire.

PROVERBS 29:17 NIV

There is a wonderful old saying in parenting that advises to "nip it in the bud." It alludes to preventing a flower bud from blooming. It's not the prettiest saying but the idea is clear—we should deal with negative situations quickly so that they do not develop into anything bigger.

Discipline is not fun for anyone, and sometimes it can be easier to take the path of least resistance. However, when we allow unwise behavior to take a foothold, it will be harder to get rid of further down the track. A little flame can set a whole forest on fire. Give the children in your care boundaries, quickly put out the small sparks, and let them know about consequences. In the long run, it will bring peace to everyone and allow you to focus on the great qualities in each child.

Heavenly Father, thank you for the children you have put in my care. Thank you that your Word gives advice on discipline and that I can be assured that showing children the right way will ultimately lead to peace for all of us.

THE GREAT RACE

Since we are surrounded by such a great cloud of witnesses, let us throw off everything that hinders and the sin that so easily entangles. And let us run with perseverance the race marked out for us, fixing our eyes on Jesus, the pioneer and perfecter of faith…. Consider him who endured such opposition from sinners, so that you will not grow weary and lose heart.

HEBREWS 12:1-3 NIV

When we think of a great running race, our imagination might take us to a well-marked Olympic track; lanes lined with incredibly fit athletes all impatient to make the next world record. In reality, our life experience probably resembles more of an unwieldy obstacle course with unfit competitors battling through hurdles, mud, ropes, and water. This isn't the race that God intended for you!

The Bible says that the race has been marked out for us and that our coach and all of our biggest fans are there. The entire crowd is chanting your name; they cheer when you race ahead, and they encourage you to get back up when you fall. Our great coach helps us get rid of all the unnecessary baggage, and encourages us as we run. When we are tired, he brings us a drink. When we are discouraged, he lets us limp alongside him for a bit. This is an endurance race, but if we can learn perseverance and fix our eyes on Jesus, we will not lose heart!

Jesus, I choose to look at you as I run this race of endurance. Give me strength in those times when I feel like giving up. Give me encouragement when I fall and need help to get back up again. Show me that it will all be worth it in the end so that I will not lose heart.

NEVER STOP

Never stop praying.
1 THESSALONIANS 5:17 NLT

What? Never stop praying? Sometimes it feels like we would be lucky if we could actually *start* praying on any given day! What if we could remind ourselves to understand prayer as simple communication with our Lord? It doesn't matter if it is on your knees, out loud, on the run, in song, or in a simple thought. Any direction of your heart and mind to the Lord is prayer.

Let's be honest, we are far more likely to call a friend when we need to talk things over than stop and offer up a quick, "I need you right now, Lord." We talk through hard decisions with those around us, but forget to get on our knees to seek God about it. Can you be intentional today to let the worries, concerns, and joys of your day be directed toward God? You may be surprised and encouraged at how effective prayer can be in your day-to-day life.

Jesus, I love you and I'm sorry that I don't spend enough time talking with you and listening for your response. Remind me of your presence throughout the day.

HIS WORK

We are not saying that we can do this work ourselves.
It is God who makes us able to do all that we do.
2 CORINTHIANS 3:5 NCV

Teachers need to be pretty organized and efficient to have a successful day in the classroom. It can be a common trap for organized people to do all of the work themselves because they don't trust others to do things exactly the right way. Even if you don't consider yourself very organized, you still have many demands that come your way. Every day is full of plans that are interrupted by the unexpected.

Have you ever tried asking God into your busy day, instead of leaving time with him to the unlikely moments of peace and quiet? You may be surprised at the way he can bring order into chaos and stillness into overwhelmed thoughts. The apostle Paul also speaks of the work involved in leading people into a relationship with Jesus. In all of the good things that God has us involved in, remember that he is the one who does the real work. Pray for his strength and guidance; he wants to help you!

Father God, I thank you that I cannot do anything in my own strength. Even when I feel like I am doing all the work, I acknowledge that you are the one behind my strength and ability to persevere. I ask for your help with all that I need to do today.

OUR OASIS

Blessed is the one who trusts in the LORD,
whose confidence is in him.
They will be like a tree planted by the water
that sends out its roots by the stream.
It does not fear when heat come;
its leaves are always green.
It has no worries in a year of drought
and never fails to bear fruit.

JEREMIAH 17:7-8 NIV

In the middle of the desert, there can be an unexpected patch of greenery, known as an oasis. It shows that there is life, which means there is most certainly water sustaining that life. Despite the arid conditions and seemingly little available nutrients, plants in an oasis can flourish.

This is how the prophet Jeremiah likens our lives in Christ, as a tree planted by the water. When all external conditions seem to be failing, the follower of Christ is sustained by their roots, established in the source of life. What are your stresses today? Do you feel like they are more than you can handle? We do not need to fear when trials come our way, and we do not need to worry about provision. Be blessed today, as you trust in the Lord and place your confidence in him.

Lord God, thank you that you give me everything I need to get through every trial and worry that I have. Help me to drink from your eternal waters so that I may flourish in times of need.

THE ETERNAL CROWN

Everyone who competes in the games goes into strict training. They do it to get a crown that will not last, but we do it to get a crown that will last forever.

1 CORINTHIANS 9:25 NIV

The Olympics have been around in various forms for centuries. Regardless of what event an athlete competes in, they spend most of their waking hours training to get in the best shape possible. It is an amazing accomplishment when an athlete wins a gold medal. They have their moment of glory from the coaches, spectators, and even peers. You may never compete in games of this scale, yet it might be encouraging to take a moment to recognize that Paul was likening our belief in Christ to this hard training that culminates in glory!

As a teacher, you know that the students who usually succeed are those who have put in the most effort, whether mental or physical. Winning the crown of eternal life will be worth all of the hard work and battles you have faced in your emotional, physical, and spiritual life. Be encouraged to keep training; keep yourself spiritually fit so that you become the best you can be in this great event of Christian living. The crown is waiting for you!

Jesus, thank you for the amazing gift of eternal life. Thank you that I don't have to train without your help. Give me grace to persevere when things get tough, and remind me that it will be worth it in the end.

HIS STORY

Let each generation tell its children of your mighty acts;
let them proclaim your power.

PSALM 145:4 NLT

Do you know the story of Goldilocks? Or the nursery rhyme "Humpty Dumpty?" Do you know how to sing "Twinkle, Twinkle Little Star"? Stories and songs like these have been passed down the generations, almost without conscious intention. The same holds true in Christianity for stories like Noah's ark, Daniel and the lion's den, and Jesus' miracle of feeding thousands with a young boy's lunch.

More astounding is that much of the world celebrates festive seasons that come from the Christian traditions of Easter and Christmas. The history of the birth and death of Jesus Christ has made its way through the generations proving that the truth and power of the gospel is still being proclaimed. Be encouraged today to remind the children in your life of the stories that reveal the truth and power of our God. Pass the story on!

Thank you, God, for your greatness and your power that has been shown through us in your stories throughout history. Thank you for the people in my life who have passed these stories down to me. Remind me to be enthusiastic about passing them to the next generation.

FOUNT OF KNOWLEDGE

*Understanding is like a fountain
which gives life to those who use it.*
PROVERBS 16:22 NCV

We might know that the sun comes up in the morning, that the moon appears at night, and that the world spins around on its axis. To make the translation from this information to knowing about seasons, tides, or gravity requires a good understanding of how it all works together. Once there is explicit understanding, humans can make discoveries, predictions, and improvements in everyday living. Teaching requires more than giving information, it requires true understanding.

The Bible can be seen as a lot of information, yet there is much life that a deeper understanding of the words can bring. Are you applying your teaching skills to your faith? Are you seeking out the truth from the information? Are you applying the truth to your life? The Word says that understanding is like a fountain that gives life. Be encouraged as you allow the fountain of understanding to bring life to your heart.

Lord, your Word is important to me. I want to understand more of the Scriptures and how you are speaking to me through them. Give me the wisdom to seek out and apply your truth in my life today.

LIGHT UP YOUR FACE!

How wonderful to be wise, to analyze and interpret things.
Wisdom lights up a person's face, softening its harshness.

ECCLESIASTES 8:1 NLT

Where would we be without the great analysts of this world? Most of science has relied on the careful contemplation, experimentation, and determination of those who want to better understand the world around them. Beyond scientific discovery, we know that God has also given us minds that can help us to understand each other.

Wisdom lights up a person's face. Think of the student who has worked so hard to understand a math problem and has finally worked out the right answer. See the face before the answer, and notice it after. This is what happens to us when we are illuminated by the truth. Be encouraged to allow God to reveal a truthful interpretation of his Word and his world, and watch it light up your life!

God, you are the almighty Creator of the heavens and the earth, and I praise you. I know that there are things in this life that are too great to understand. Help me to interpret the truth in the things that I can. Brighten my face with your wisdom.

UNTO THE LORD

The LORD takes pleasure in those who fear him,
in those who hope in his steadfast love.
PSALM 147:11 ESV

Eric Liddell, a missionary to China, competed in the 1924 Olympic games for the 400-meter dash. His sister, whom he worked with at a mission in Scotland, was concerned his pursuit of running would distract him from the Lord. But Eric said that he felt the pleasure of God when he ran. Even before the games began, Liddell's commitment to the Lord was tested. His qualifying race was on a Sunday, which was widely accepted as the day of rest for Christians. In godly fear and adherence to God's command to keep the Sabbath holy, he announced that he was unable to compete in the race.

Eric put his hope and confidence in the Lord, and in the end, a colleague allowed Eric to take his place in a race that was on a Thursday. Liddell ran with his head lifted, experiencing the delight of his heavenly Father as he crossed the finish line and won. Winning was only part of the ecstatic moment; the lasting reward was knowing God's pleasure as he ran unto the Lord rather than unto himself.

Father, help me fear you and follow your commands above any other so that I feel your pleasure over my life and remain victorious. I want all that I do today to be unto you. Thank you for your mercy, which is new every morning. Today, I put my hope in you alone.

GIVING HONOR

"Those who honor me I will honor."
1 Samuel 2:30 niv

Creating a culture of honor in our school classrooms is as critical as teaching students how to read. One way we honor others is by listening. We can cultivate a climate of attentive listening to parents, teachers, other leaders, and classmates, which will then help students hear from God and honor him.

Teachers can provide opportunities each day to train their students to listen and honor others. Techniques such as reading aloud with follow up questions, listening drills with step-by-step instructions, or taking turns asking questions about a particular subject, are all-important lessons of respect and honor. Our students can start to learn honor for God by learning how to honor you, their parents, and their classmates. Honoring God and others is the pathway to success.

Father, I want to honor you in all that I do. Help me to follow your ways to create a godly culture of honor in my classroom. May each of my students understand the importance of honor.

OUR PRESENT HOPE

Through Christ you have come to trust in God. And you have placed your faith and hope in God because he raised Christ from the dead and gave him great glory.
1 PETER 1:21 NLT

Our present hope, as sons and daughters of the King, is that God raised Christ Jesus from the dead and has seated him at the right hand of the Father. From this place, Jesus makes intercession for us. He has also raised us up to sit with him in heavenly places! Assured of this hope, we can daily sit with Jesus and agree with him in prayer.

We can be confident that Jesus will perfect all that concerns us as we pray in unity with him for his purposes to be established. Jesus can and will do above and beyond what we ask or imagine, according to the power that works in us. As we let the Holy Spirit take the lead and come into agreement with Jesus for what he desires to see in our schools and community, we will experience breakthrough in areas that seemed impossible. Place your faith and hope in God, because if God is for you, no one can be against you!

Father, thank you that you provide all that I need. I entrust myself to you. Lead me on your straight path and deliver me from evil. You are my hope.

VALUABLE LIKE NO OTHER

He gave some as… teachers, for the equipping of the saints for the work of service, to the building up of the body of Christ.

EPHESIANS 4:11-12 NASB

Teachers are valuable. A key role of a teacher is to help students see their intrinsic value, which builds them up and helps them fulfill God's purpose. We all need to know that our lives have a special purpose. It is what gives motivation to and go through the discipline of hard work. Our only requirement is to be and do the best we can. There is no one else in the world exactly like us.

We do not have to compare or compete for our sense of importance; rather, we welcome collaboration with others who bring their unique skill sets. Providing encouragement to students publicly and privately reinforces the message that they are valuable. It motivates them to continue. Who can you encourage today by letting them know their value?

Father, help me nurture each of my students and equip them to do their best work. Help me see the unique talents of each one. Give me your insights of how to cultivate and maintain a learning environment that builds up rather than compares. Thank you for this opportunity to teach. It is a great honor and blessing.

HOPE IN GOD

Why am I discouraged? Why is my heart so sad?
I will put my hope in God! I will praise him again—
my Savior and my God!

PSALM 42:11 NLT

It is sad to see the way we hurt each other. We are surrounded by sickness and death. The immorality we witness in human trafficking, pornography, and corruption is overwhelming. But God is good and faithful. We have an opportunity each day to mold a new generation to put their hope in God, who holds the whole world in his hands.

Each child is precious to God. It is critical that we don't allow the evil in this world, stress, or the monotony of life to weigh on us. We need to put our hope in God and praise him for what he has done and is able to do. As their teachers, we guide them into a new way—the only way, truth, and life, which is Jesus Christ. There are plenty of reasons to be sad and upset; be encouraged to hope in the goodness of God.

Jesus, quicken my soul with your presence and let me experience your light. I give my sadness and frustration to you. I will put my hope in you and keep praising your name.

GIVING IN SECRET

"When you give to the needy, do not let your left hand know what your right hand is doing, so that your giving may be in secret. Then your Father, who sees what is done in secret, will reward you."

MATTHEW 6:3-4 NIV

How many things do you do that no one sees? Teachers invest countless hours preparing for classes, doing work that is not compensated, working with students behind the scenes, and buying supplies out of their own resources.

God sees all that you do each day. He sees when you reach out to a needy student, encourage a colleague, and sacrifice so someone else can benefit. Your Father in heaven sees all that you do in secret and is storing up a reward for you. When you give in secret, you experience joy and freedom. You are no longer held captive by possessions. You do not become puffed up by your talents. Your heart is filled with gratitude. Don't get tired of doing good. Continue to do your work unto the Lord and ask him to bless the work of your hands, even if no one is watching.

Lord, thank you for seeing all that I do in secret. I do all of it for you, Jesus. Receive my giving as an offering of worship. Strengthen my hands to continue to give to the needy and to help the weak.

A SERVANT'S HONOR

"My Father will honor the one who serves me."
JOHN 12:26 NIV

Teachers are some of the greatest servants in the world. Some teach for decades, serving hundreds or thousands of students, and finish their career with very few recognizing their extravagant commitment and sacrifice. But God will honor those who serve him.

In God's eyes, the integrity or honor of a person has much greater value than works or gifts. As you have taught and acted honorably, know that God honors you. He sees your heart and your well-meaning intentions. Keep this in mind today as you take the form of a servant. The Father spoke publicly from heaven about Jesus, "This is my beloved Son, in whom I am well pleased." Hear God honor you in the same way, saying that you are his beloved child, and that he is so pleased with you.

Lord, give me a servant's heart. My heart is to serve you and your kingdom. Thank you, Father, for the honor you give to me at home, in my classroom, with colleagues, and with friends. Help me to honor you with my words and actions today as I serve.

FROM GOD'S PERSPECTIVE

"God does not show favoritism but accepts from every nation the one who fears him and does what is right."
ACTS 10:34–35 NIV

In Acts 10, the Bible records that the Holy Spirit urged Peter to doubt nothing and go with three men sent to bring him to Caesarea to meet Cornelius, a Roman centurion. Cornelius had the reputation among the nation of the Jews of being a just man who feared God. His prayers, fasting, and giving to the poor were remembered by the Lord, and he was encouraged by Peter's obedience.

Sometimes we judge people by outward appearance. God always looks at the heart. He looked at Cornelius' heart, and he sees the hearts of those around you. Don't get stuck in your judgments about people. Heed the voice of God and follow his lead instead.

Father, give me divine encounters with those whose actions are acceptable and remembered before your throne. Thank you for making a way through the death and resurrection of Jesus for all people from every nation to be accepted into the family of God.

PREPARING A PLACE

*"There is more than enough room in my Father's home.
If this were not so, would I have told you that I am going
to prepare a place for you? When everything is ready,
I will come and get you, so that you will always be
with me where I am."*
JOHN 14:2-3 NLT

Jesus promised us an eternal dwelling that he is preparing for us. His preparations are unseen, yet he is definite in his plan and unlimited in his creativity to make it the most suitable for us. Just as Jesus prepares a place for us, teachers can prepare and cultivate safe and enriching learning environments for students.

No detail is too small for God to personalize, and everything he does is done with excellence. We can do the same with his divine guidance. Jesus promised the Holy Spirit would be our helper to teach and provide counsel to us. His creative power is with us every day, and we can welcome him to direct every step to prepare an environment where students can encounter God's love.

Jesus, thank you for your promise that you are preparing a place for me in your kingdom. Please help me do the same for the students you have entrusted to me to teach. Remind me, Holy Spirit, that you desire to help me plan and prepare as Jesus is doing.

INCREASE SENSITIVITY

Share each other's burdens,
and in this way obey the law of Christ.
GALATIANS 6:2 NLT

When your toe hurts, your head hurts. When your back hurts, your entire midsection hurts. This is how we need to be when other members of the body of Christ are experiencing pain. When a widow is mourning for her husband or a parent is in despair over the loss of a child, we should be in pain also.

Just as our natural body parts try to compensate for pain in other parts, we are to attempt to lessen the pain of other members of the body of Christ. This necessitates sensitivity to others. Teachers have the wonderful and weighty responsibility to be aware of our students' problems. Do not be hesitant to inquire or reach out if you sense a student has a burden today. When we reach out to help someone, we are following our Lord and fulfilling his law of love.

Lord, increase my sensitivity to those I encounter today. Keep my heart ready to reach out and be your hands and feet of comfort today.

OCTOBER

Be patient and stand firm,
because the Lord's coming is near.

JAMES 5:8 NIV

MY SUSTAINER, PROTECTOR, AND HELPER

The LORD is my strength and my shield;
my heart trusts in him, and he helps me.
My heart leaps for joy,
and with my song I praise him.

PSALM 28:7 NIV

Life gives us many reasons to trust God. Perhaps you have gone without food, been terribly sick, lived in a foreign land, or become a new parent. You may even find that teaching requires a lot of trust in him. In times of hardship, we trust God, and he helps us. He comes through and our heart sings to him because of his great kindness toward us. We can be confident in his desire and ability to intervene in situations.

God alone is our sustainer, protector, and helper. We can praise him even before we see how he orchestrates his solution because he is dependable and worthy of our trust. Often God uses others to meet our needs. They freely give because they have received. It's one of the wonderful ways that God's kingdom works. Are you willing to receive his help today?

Lord, you are my strength and my shield; my heart trusts in you alone. Thank you for your constant help. I lift up my voice and hands to bless you. You are good and I will sing with my whole heart.

OUR GUIDE

*The true children of God are those who
let God's Spirit lead them.*

ROMANS 8:14 NCV

Although we are teachers, we often find that our students teach us! Children can be very in touch with what God has put in their hearts. They don't get stuck trying to figure out everything in their minds. They instinctively know what is true and what is a lie.

When a teacher asked a nine-year-old girl whom she and her family worship, she lit up with her answer, "Well, I guess I worship myself!" This child knew the answer, but she had not yet chosen to follow God's Spirit. Let's be true children of God who enter the kingdom of heaven and follow his Spirit.

Father, I want to be a true child of God, letting your Spirit lead me. I want to follow the Holy Spirit as I interact with others today. Teach me your ways that are higher than mine and let your Spirit be evident in my life.

RICH PROVISION

As for the rich in this present age, charge them not to be haughty, nor to set their hopes on the uncertainty of riches, but on God, who richly provides us with everything to enjoy.

1 TIMOTHY 6:17 ESV

We have a tendency to rely upon our finances to sustain us. We have endowment funds, property, and investments to give us security. Our desire to be wealthy can often come from forgetting that our Father in heaven has all the resources in the universe. He is the one who provides. The apostle Paul warns us to not trust in riches because they are uncertain and perishable.

George Mueller, an evangelist in the 1800s, started fifty orphanages without asking anyone except the Lord for support. He tells of the time that he had three hundred children that needed lunch and they had no food. At twelve noon, a baker showed up at the door as well as a milkman who each had enough provision for all the children.

You might feel as though you have many needs. Instead of setting your hope on riches, look to a loving Father who richly provides us with everything to enjoy.

Jesus, thank you for the many good gifts that have come from your hand. I set my hope on you, not on riches that are uncertain. Regardless of great wealth or lack of it, help me to remain humble, willing to share what I have to meet the needs of others.

ABUNDANT GRACE

*God's law was given so that all people could see how
sinful they were. But as people sinned more and more,
God's wonderful grace became more abundant.*
ROMANS 5: 20 NLT

God's grace is amazing. Think of your life before you
became a follower of Jesus. Sin controlled you. You had no
certainty of an eternal future. When you chose to follow Jesus,
grace revealed your right standing with God and the gift of
eternal life. You couldn't save yourself, so God stepped in to
save you. This is amazing grace.

God has this same grace for your students and others at
your school. It will help the blind to see and lead them into
a relationship with God. When you are overwhelmed by the
sin you see around you, know that God's wonderful grace is
greater. It can bring anyone into right standing with God.

**Jesus, thank you for your amazing grace in my life. Where
sin and death abounds in my school, I ask that your grace
would become even more abundant and lead many into a
relationship with Jesus Christ.**

FORGIVING LIKE GOD

As far as the east is from the west,
So far has he removed our transgressions from us.
PSALM 103:12 NIV

The writer of this psalm understood the forgiveness of God because he experienced it. God forgave his adultery, deceit, and murder—transgressions with heavy consequences. Knowing that he had been forgiven, David also learned to forgive others, including his son who betrayed him.

The greatest example of forgiveness was demonstrated by Jesus, who took every sin, past, present, and future, upon himself. Can you imagine? Every sin, for every person, for all time. He removed them completely, as far as the east is from the west. If God forgives our sin and willingly paid so great a price for this grace, we can do the same with a troublesome student, a frustrating colleague, or a difficult parent. Follow God's example today and forgive.

Father, thank you for forgiving me and removing my sin completely from me. Forgive me for my unwillingness to extend mercy to others. Soften my heart and help me to forgive. I let go of the hurt and injustice and trust you to make things right in this situation.

TASTE GOD'S GOODNESS

Taste and see that the LORD is good;
blessed is the one who takes refuge in him.

PSALM 34:8 NIV

The psalmist chose a very artistic and unusual way to say we can experience God: through taste. How can we taste God? Possibly the overwhelming goodness of an experience with God is so great that our senses retain its flavor long after the experience is only a memory. When we truly taste God, we know that he is good. Many have a belief in an avenging and critical God who is waiting to punish us for breaking his law. This is a false belief based upon a wrong perception of God.

God wants us to know him and experience his goodness. When we encounter difficulties and run to him for refuge, we have the opportunity to taste how good he is as he fills our hearts with his love. Remember God's goodness in your life today and savor it. Then help those around you to taste and see that God is good.

Father, I want to taste and see your goodness. Remove any barriers that are keeping me from a greater revelation of Jesus. May the fullness of who you are be passed on to each of my students today.

LOOK AT THE HEART

The LORD does not see as man sees; for man looks at the outward appearance, but the LORD looks at the heart.

1 SAMUEL 16:7 NKJV

As teachers, we don't typically have a choice of who comes into our classrooms. We don't always have a choice of who comes into our lives. We can be quick to judge others based on the way someone looks or talks, but there is so much more to each person than that.

If we don't take the time to look past the outer appearance, we'll never uncover the true person hidden inside their hearts. It might be difficult at times, but it's important to set aside what you see and tune in to what's really going on beneath the surface. We can't know what someone really needs from us by looking on the outside. When we are patient enough to unearth the true person inside, then we can really love our students and begin to change their lives.

Lord, help me to look past my first impressions. Give me the patience to find out what's hidden in each person's heart. Help me to love each of my students equally, despite my own personal comfort or preference.

BELONGING

I have redeemed you;
I have called you by name;
you are Mine!

ISAIAH 43:1 NASB

Belonging to someone means to be earmarked, to be set apart, to have a purpose. When Jesus redeemed us, he bought us from sin. He rightfully owns us, and with that ownership comes his purposes, his delight, and his covering.

It's easy to feel like we are not making a difference. We feel like our purpose has become watered down by the mundane daily responsibilities we face. But we are set apart and chosen to fulfill a vision that's bigger than what we can see. By remaining constantly faithful in ordinary tasks, we are unknowingly completing a destiny that's magnificent. We have been named, bought, and assigned. Our purpose is important and we must never doubt it.

God, help me to be consistent in the purpose you've marked for me. I get tired of the daily routine. I lose sight of my own exciting destiny amidst mundane tasks like grading papers and preparing lessons. Whether I stop to think it or not, I'm shaping lives. Help me never to doubt the importance of that purpose.

DEAL TRUTHFULLY

Those who deal truthfully are His delight.

PROVERBS 12:22 NKJV

We are creatures of resolve. We want to see solutions. We feel in control when we've seen a situation from start to finish. Sometimes the most direct path to resolution is to cut corners, to do something less than honestly. But is it ever worth it?

When we deal with people or situations honestly, we actually bring delight to the Lord. He takes pleasure in our efforts to honor the truth, and he's glorified in our dealings. It doesn't matter how much simpler dishonesty might seem on the outside, it will never pay off in the long run. We will be left with regret and the dissatisfaction of knowing that we didn't please God with our actions. Even when it is hard, we have to deal with every situation presented to us with honesty and integrity.

Lord God, I want to walk in your truth. I want to delight you. I want you to look at how I live my life and be honored with my actions. Help me to stop when I am about to move forward in dishonesty and make the necessary changes to delight you with truth.

QUICKER IN LOVE

Be not quick in your spirit to become angry,
for anger lodges in the heart of fools.

ECCLESIASTES 7:9 ESV

Anger is an easy emotion. It comes far more naturally than patience, self-control, and love. But the problem with anger is that it's persistent. Once we allow ourselves to go past the point of irritation into being infuriated, we've gone down a path that's hard to turn back from. It begins to permeate everything.

Anger lodges itself in our hearts and taints our relationships. No matter how hard we try to hide it, it will come out in the way we speak and interact. We must spend time in the presence of God, learning from his slowness to anger. Only by his Spirit can we train our hearts to be quicker in love than they are in resentment.

Lord, help me to examine my relationships and identify the places where irritation is beginning to take hold. If I have allowed anger to rise up toward anyone in my life, I ask that you would give me the strength to do what it will take to resolve that anger and move forward in love.

TAUGHT TO TEACH

He must have a strong belief in the trustworthy message
he was taught; then he will be able to encourage others
with wholesome teaching and show those who oppose
it where they are wrong.
TITUS 1:9 NLT

No one teaches without first being taught. We spend our entire lives learning, and then, in turn, learning how to pass those things down. Only when we become fully convinced of what we've learned do we truly become capable of teaching with conviction, power, and impact.

Our strength in belief comes with dedicated learning. It comes with daily sitting at the feet of God, immersed in his Word, and absorbing his wisdom. It isn't a one-time education; it's a constant reliance. We must step daily into his presence and spend time learning his message before we step out into the world to teach and encourage others.

Lord, reveal my own need for your wisdom. Help me to long for your presence in such a way that I cannot start my day without stopping and learning from your Word. I know that I can only reach my full potential as a teacher when I become a persistent student of you.

SOURCE OF JOY

*Surely you have granted him unending blessings
and made him glad with the joy of your presence.*

PSALM 21:6 NIV

We are usually quick to present our struggles to God. He is our help in times of trouble and we often lean into him when we are at our weakest. As we look to him to be our source of strength, we must remember that he is also our source of joy. While he is close to us in our sadness, he is also at the center of our greatest happiness.

There's something powerful about recognizing our blessings, naming our joys, and identifying where they came from. When we give glory to God for the good things in our lives, we find even more gladness in his presence, because he is good to us. When we label the blessings he's poured out on us, we cannot help but be left in wonder of his faithfulness to our hearts.

Thank you, Lord, for your goodness to me. I don't deserve the many blessings in my life but you continue to give them anyway. Your presence makes me glad. You could have made me feel any emotion in your presence, but you chose to give me joy. Thank you.

SHARED LIFE

Bear one another's burdens, and so fulfill the law of Christ.
GALATIANS 6:2 ESV

God didn't create us to walk through life alone. He specifically designed us to live in relationship with others who would share life with us. By coming alongside someone else, we can amplify their joy and lessen their sorrow simply by being in the midst of their experience.

Students will enter your classroom daily with all sorts of burdens weighing on their shoulders. Some you may know about, some you can only guess. Regardless, you can lessen their load by being patient, kind, and understanding. Remember that behind every set of slumped shoulders and each bad attitude is a heart affected by human imperfection. Every one of us is navigating our way through difficult circumstances to find the love and peace of God.

God, help me show your love to my students by sharing their burdens. I know that each of them come from imperfect families and live through difficult circumstances. Even though I'm not perfect either, I can show your light to them while they are with me.

FACES UNCOVERED

Our faces, then, are not covered. We all show the
Lord's glory, and we are being changed to be like him.
This change in us brings ever greater glory,
which comes from the Lord, who is the Spirit.

2 CORINTHIANS 3:18 NCV

The glory of God is so powerful, and so unlike anything on this earth, that when Moses would step into God's presence, he would have to veil his face before coming back down from the mountain where he met with God. The glory of God was so powerful that not just anyone could look on it at any given moment. When Jesus came, he shifted everything about how we experience glory. He gave every believer instant, uninhibited access to the glorious presence of the Father.

When we've been with God through worship and reading his Word, we don't have to cover our faces afterward. We are able to step away and carry the glory that we've just encountered with us. We reveal his character as we interact with the world. Those around us are touched by his presence in us.

Lord God, thank you for choosing to reveal your glory through me. I don't always stop to feel the gravity of the fact that I can step into your presence daily. Help me to be faithful to spend time with you so that the changes you are making in my life will be evident to the world.

LIKE LITTLE CHILDREN

*"Unless you change and become like little children,
you will never enter the kingdom of heaven."*

MATTHEW 18:3 NIV

It's always interesting to see how opposite God's kingdom is from ours. He tells us to become like little children to enter his heavenly kingdom. Here, children are the lowest of our social system. They are viewed as the least intelligent and least capable. Still, God says to become like them to be with him.

Children may not be capable of making weighty decisions, but they are capable of keen faith. They may not know how to prepare themselves for life's hard realities, but they are able to hope for things that are beyond imagination. They may not understand the complexity of relationships, but they do understand pure love. While we have many qualifications that we feel are important, there are three things that God tells us are most important: faith, hope, and love.

Holy Spirit, return to me my childlike faith to trust you more. Remind me what it is to hope without fear. Restore my ability to love purely without hesitation. Change me to become like a child again so that I can enter your kingdom and know you fully.

LEARN FAITHFULLY, TEACH WISELY

"These words which I command you today shall be in your heart. You shall teach them diligently to your children, and shall talk of them when you sit in your house, when you walk by the way, when you lie down, and when you rise up."

DEUTERONOMY 6:6-7 NKJV

It's easy to get comfortable with the Bible. We become used to it, accustomed to its availability in our lives. The power of the Word of God, however, is not to be underestimated. When we dig deep into the words and allow our eyes to be opened and our souls to be changed, it causes a ripple effect in our lives. Truth flows out of us when we speak, love pours out when we interact with people, and wisdom comes naturally.

Putting the Word into your heart must become a practice. It can't be a one time or occasional thing. Only when you diligently, daily, draw strength from time in the Bible can it become a consistent hunger. As you pour truth into your own soul, truth will spill out of you onto your students and your community.

Hide your Word in my heart, Lord. Help me to absorb your words as I read them so your truth will flow out of me. Give me the strength to learn faithfully so I can teach wisely.

FEET SECURE

The LORD will be your confidence,
And will keep your foot from being caught.

PROVERBS 3:26 NKJV

Have you ever tried to walk across a river, balancing from one half-wet rock to another? You tentatively reach one foot forward; testing it before resting your weight, hoping the footing is secure. Your arms fly out to the sides as you check yourself, not wanting to fall into the water. You take every step this way, unsure which rocks are firm and trustworthy, and which might be slippery and deceiving.

In life, we second-guess ourselves daily. We aren't sure if the next step we're taking is the right one, and whether our decision will be met with confirmation or regret. We never see the full picture, never know if we chose the right rock until we're standing there, putting our weight on places untested. When we commit our way to the Lord, he gives us the confidence we lack. He doesn't always stop us from choosing the slippery rock, but he will keep us from falling off. By trusting his Word and following his leading, we can walk forward confidently in the knowledge that our paths are protected and our feet are secure.

Thank you, Lord that you go before me, preparing my way. Help me to step out in my decisions in confident faith, not worrying about the outcome but trusting in your grace.

EXCELLENT WORK

Whatever your hand finds to do, do it with all your might.
ECCLESIASTES 9:10 NIV

God values excellence. He's a God of perfect creation who didn't stop to rest until he had observed his work and was pleased with what he had done. His example shows us how important it is that we take pride in the work we set our hands to.

No matter what it is we do, it's easy to lower our standards. We see those around us putting in less effort than we do, and we realize that we can get by quite well without even attempting perfection. With all the countless demands placed on us, and the tempting distractions around us, it takes true discipline to stay on task. When we focus ourselves on the work in front of us, and refuse to rest until we are satisfied with the job that we've done, we honor God in our work and make the greatest possible impact on the world around us.

Lord, give me discipline in my work and the focus to work excellently for you. Help me to remember that no matter how difficult my job may be, you will give me the strength to complete it well.

SWEET SLEEP

When you lie down, you will not be afraid;
when you lie down, your sleep will be sweet.
PROVERBS 3:24 NIV

Fear comes most readily at night: when we are lying in the dark, unable to see the impracticality of what scares us. We lose ourselves in thoughts of "what if," and wonder about troubles that haven't even happened. It's easy to lose ourselves in the hours of blank space, and sleep escapes us in favor of a racing mind. But when morning comes, we instantly recognize the truth and our worries dissolve with the light.

When you put your trust in the Lord, he becomes your constant light. He becomes your morning and your truth and your peace. In the dark, when worries wake you and troubled thoughts come, call on his name. Let him be the light of truth to your heart. Sleep sweetly wrapped in his perfect love which casts out all fear.

Thank you, Lord, that you protect my sleep. Thank you that you care enough about my heart to cast out even my most irrational fears. Thank you that your desire for me is to be brave and to feel peaceful and loved.

PRIORITY OF LOVE

Don't love money; be satisfied with what you have.
For God has said, "I will never fail you.
I will never abandon you."

<small>HEBREWS 13:5 NLT</small>

Whatever we love, we prioritize. Our deepest love naturally becomes our strongest pursuit. In life, it's easy for our loves to become imbalanced. We need money for so many things that it's natural for us to become overwhelmed by its necessity. If we could recognize and absorb the reality that God will always meet our needs, perhaps money wouldn't be such an all-consuming pursuit. We would relax ourselves in the sweetness of trust and believe that as we chase after God, he will take care of us. He doesn't abandon us and he won't leave us destitute.

While chasing after money and the love of it may make us comfortable, or satisfy us temporarily, it will never save our souls. We must adjust our love and refocus ourselves on Christ. Once that order is restored, will we be able to live to our full potential and at complete peace.

Lord, search my heart. Help me recognize any area in which I've begun to prioritize something above you. Help me evaluate my actions and my pursuits and determine whether I am motivated by money, or by trust in you and your purposes.

BROKEN SPIRIT

My sacrifice, O God, is a broken spirit;
a broken and contrite heart you, God, will not despise.

PSALM 51:17 NIV

Do you ever come to God feeling absolutely broken? You lay your soul out before him and you feel in that moment like you have nothing eloquent to say and nothing beautiful to present. Whether you're coming from sin, or defeat, or sadness and hardship, you step into his presence feeling empty and tired.

God glories in our honesty. When we come to him with nothing, vulnerable and without pretense, he stoops low and is near to us. He doesn't ask that we rise to meet him; he meets us where we are and lifts us. It doesn't matter how broken your heart is; he is able to heal. It doesn't matter how shocking your sin, or how devastating your sorrow; there is a grace giver and a comforter.

Lord God, there are highs and lows in this life. There are days when I feel strong and happy and proud. There are days when I feel empty and weak and in need. Thank you, God, that you are my safe place no matter how I come to you.

EASY GRACE

If anyone is caught in any trespass… restore such a one in a spirit of gentleness; each one looking to yourself, so that you too will not be tempted.

GALATIANS 6:1 NASB

We see our students through everything—the good, bad, happy, and hard. When they come into our classroom, they are coming into our sphere of influence. The words we speak and even the emotion we use will affect their spirits. When your student does something wrong, you are usually the first line of defense, the first one to notice, or the first one told. What you do with their weakness will likely determine when and if they rise in strength.

Young minds are easily molded. The wrongdoing of one of your students likely has a long and involved story behind it. Take the time to unlock the start of the sin before you react too harshly to the situation. We've been treated with undeserved grace in our lives and to extend the same grace to others is our privilege.

Thank you, God, for your grace toward me. It's easy to expect grace, but not always easy to offer it. Give me your heart toward my students so that no matter how difficult it might feel in my flesh, it's always easy for my spirit to give grace.

GENTLE HEIRS

"Blessed are the gentle, for they shall inherit the earth."
MATTHEW 5:5 NASB

When you think of what it means to be gentle, what comes to mind? Perhaps the way you cradle a new baby. There is a certain softness or tenderness. What about someone who is meek and mild mannered? Sometimes, without even realizing it, our minds equate gentleness with weakness.

When God says that the gentle will inherit the earth, it makes us stop and take a second look at the word. We would imagine that someone who would inherit the earth would be bold, strong, loud, and confident. The way that God sets up his system, however, is immensely opposite from ours. Those who are gentle, who are quick to listen, slow to speak, and slow to anger; those who are tender in their interactions with others—they will become the heirs to the earth. God trusts his kingdom with this type of person.

God, make me gentle. Make me gracious. Let me be a light to those around me by my submission to your Spirit and my actions that point back to your grace. Give me the strength to be gentle and the wisdom to stand firm.

HEARTS FULL OF TREASURE

*"A good man's speech reveals
the rich treasures within him."*
MATTHEW 12:35 TLB

You can tell a lot about a person from what they say. Some people don't say much, but when they do speak, you are left thinking about their words long after they've said them. Whenever wisdom flows out from someone, you know there is more where it came from. Wise words are spoken from good hearts. And good hearts are developed by minds that are continually exposed to the truth.

It is important to control what we say. We are told in the book of James just how powerful the tongue is. It can start a fire, or calm a storm. It can build a person up or tear them down. But we can't control what we say unless we are diligently controlling the condition of our hearts. Only by hiding the Word of God in our hearts can we accumulate treasure within us.

Heavenly Father, keep me in your Word. I want the words that I speak to reveal a heart of rich treasure, not a mind full of junk. Give me diligence in what I'm putting into my heart and mind so that when I speak to others, I am sharing value with them instead of words that have no lasting benefit.

UNDER QUALIFIED

I myself am convinced, my brothers and sisters, that you yourselves are full of goodness, filled with knowledge and competent to instruct one another.

ROMANS 15:14 NIV

Do you ever feel under qualified to teach? Do you ever stand in front of the class and wonder, *What am I doing? What do I have to offer?* When God decided to make teaching a gift, he did it because he knew that learning from one another would become our great asset and encouragement.

There is something powerful about teaching from your weakness. When you connect with your students on their level—by being you in all of your imperfection and failing—they begin to see the potential in themselves to help others. They realize that they don't have to reach some great height in order to do good for the world. They can offer what they already have, with kindness in their hearts and confidence in God's perfect plan for them.

God, I don't always feel qualified to teach. In fact, most days I feel the opposite. But I do know that you have given me a passion for teaching. I know that you awoke a desire in me to help others by sharing what I know with them. Help me not to doubt what you've led me to do.

GIFT OF WISDOM

If any of you lacks wisdom, you should ask God,
who gives generously to all without finding fault,
and it will be given to you.

JAMES 1:5 NIV

We are all faced, daily, with decisions and situations that we have no idea what to do with. We have to make choices that carry a lot of weight, or give advice that we know our students will follow. We freeze because we never want to go down the wrong path or say the wrong thing, but we don't always know what the right thing looks like.

God is clear on this. If we don't have the wisdom we need, he will give it to us. Asking for wisdom is the first step. We need to be able to admit that we don't have the answers and acknowledge that without God, we'd be lost. He says that he will give wisdom generously. He doesn't find fault with our lack of wisdom, he resolves it. The next time you are faced with a hard task, stop and ask the Lord for his wisdom. His Spirit will guide you rightly.

Lord, give me your wisdom. I don't have all the answers and I don't even have to pretend that I do. I just have to ask you for wisdom, and you will give it to me. Thank you.

PATIENT TEACHER

Guide me in your truth and teach me,
for you are God my Savior,
and my hope is in you all day long.
PSALM 25:5 NIV

When you are teaching a student to read, do you just hand them a sheet of paper with words on it and ask them to let you know when they've mastered it? Of course not. You sit down next to them and show them each letter, one by one, reading it out for them and showing them your mouth as you form the sound. You show them pictures so their brains will connect the words with the objects. You work with them, painstakingly at times, dedicating yourself to their process.

In the same way, God doesn't just give us his truth in his Word and then leave us to figure it out. He guides and teaches us how to follow it and shows us gently with his Spirit when we are wrong. We can have constant hope in his goodness because he's proven himself to be a patient teacher. He doesn't expect the impossible from us. He does the impossible for us and brings us with him.

Thank you, God, for being my patient teacher. Thank you for always guiding me through my life and showing me how to follow your Word. I have so much hope knowing that I am never on my own.

EVIL PRACTICE

Do not lie to one another, since you laid aside the old self with its evil practices, and have put on the new self who is being renewed to a true knowledge.

COLOSSIANS 3:9-10 NASB

Honesty is the best policy, right? We say that all the time, and in theory it makes a lot of sense. But when we are right in the thick of a complicated situation, honesty can seem almost impossible. The truth can hurt and we might worry what will happen to a relationship if we lay it all out there in the light.

Lying is something that God takes very seriously. He refers to it as an "evil practice." It's no small offense. Our new self in Christ is defined by the freedom of truth, and to continue to lie once we've put on Christ is a complete denial of the work he's doing in us. Lying will hurt us and those around us more deeply than the truth ever will. Only once the truth is uncovered can healing begin.

God, give me the discipline it takes to be truthful. I don't want to lie to those I love and ultimately hurt them. I am so thankful for the renewing work that you're doing in my life and I know that truthfulness is a part of that. Make me more like you.

SPIRITUAL DNA

*"To all who did accept him and believe in him
he gave the right to become children of God."*
JOHN 1:12 NCV

When a child is born into a family, there is nothing that can make that child not belong. There might be things that threaten to come between the child and their family, like separation, broken relationships, or distance. Despite separation, family members are inherently a part of each other; they are part of the same DNA.

When God says that we can become his children, he is acknowledging that it is our DNA. It is something that we are entitled to. This is an inherent truth that cannot be changed. Our acceptance of him secures our place in his family. Nothing can change that—not the separation of sin, not the doubt that comes quietly, not the world's theories or arguments. Our place as children of God is secure.

Thank you, Lord for the security that comes in knowing that you've given me the right to be your child. No matter what I've come up against in life, you've extended grace, love, and a place in your family.

BRING CALM

Fools give full vent to their rage,
but the wise bring calm in the end.
PROVERBS 29:11 NIV

We are all going to feel angry. We are constantly placed in situations that stretch us, push us, and frustrate us. Anger starts inside a person but it doesn't have the power to damage others until it's been released. Unfortunately, once anger has been given a voice, those around us feel it and are driven by it.

In the face of a rising temper, we can breathe calm. Wisdom is finding a way to invite peace into the most tumultuous moments. When we can bring that calm to our students, to our classrooms, then we are able to introduce an atmosphere that will ultimately change their lives. It is revolutionary to choose peace over an argument and humility over being right. You will demonstrate that walking in wisdom brings a more satisfactory outcome than giving in to anger.

God, I want wisdom and peace to reign in my heart, in my life, and in my classroom. I want to show those who look up to me that seeking your wisdom will always be the best course of action. Give me the strength not to fail in front of my students and the grace to bring calm.

OUTDONE BY LOVE

Love one another with mutual affection;
outdo one another in showing honor.

ROMANS 12:10 NRSV

We are naturally competitive. We compare ourselves all too easily, and where we compare, we will ultimately compete. In theory, we want those around us to do well; we don't consciously wish ill on others, but when we begin to feel threatened by someone's success, appearance, or the attention they receive, we can go very quickly from being happy for them to being jealous.

God calls us to the type of love for one another that is greater than competition. The kind of love where your heart is softened. You are happy for them whether or not you think their life is better than yours. The concept that God presents of outdoing one another with honor is a beautiful calling. When we make it our goal to honor others more than they honor us, we begin a movement of love and goodness that will gain momentum.

God, give me the strength to love others even when I'm fighting jealousy over what they have or what they've done. I want to be someone who honors others and loves affectionately.

NOVEMBER

All the promises of God
in Him are Yes,
and in Him Amen,
to the glory of God through us.

2 CORINTHIANS 1:20 NKJV

GIVE HOPE

Hope does not disappoint, because the love of God has been poured out in our hearts by the Holy Spirit who was given to us.

ROMANS 5:5 NKJV

Imagine you are underwater. You are completely disoriented and you can't tell which way is up. You have lost the ability to determine how deep you are and where the surface is. You become frantic, desperately needing oxygen and wanting light. Now imagine that you know, no matter how dark it is and how hard it is to breathe, that you will resurface in two minutes. You know that as long as you can hold your breath and hang on for just two more minutes, you will be able to come to the surface and breathe again.

Hope is like oxygen. Having something to look forward to can make even the darkest days bearable. Knowing there is an end in sight makes every mountain easier to climb and every valley easier to pass through. Every day, when you interact with your students, you have the opportunity to give hope. You have the ability to be the reason they keep fighting to breathe. You can give them the sliver of light that will keep them going through the hard times. No matter how hard it may be some days, always give hope.

Thank you, God, for hope. Life can be rough for me sometimes, and leave me wondering if I'll ever resurface. Your hope is what keeps me going and helps me to know that things will be all right.

DELIGHT IN THE LAW

Your laws are my treasure;
they are my heart's delight.
PSALM 119:111 NLT

The words *law* and *delight* seem like they should be opposites. Law makes us think of stringency, of rules and punishment. When we truly come to understand the law of God, we will also come to love it. The law is not in place to bind us, but to free us.

How can we teach our students to treasure God's laws? How can we inspire them to love truth, kindness, and integrity? Only by teaching them to love the lawgiver. Not until you come to trust the one who put the law in place will you be able to follow it joyfully. When you understand that laws exist to protect you, to guide you, and to give you a better life, you develop a hunger to learn the law and to know it thoroughly so that you can obey it well.

Lord God, give me a delight for your law. Give me a better understanding of the goodness of your parameters, knowing that you wouldn't have put them in place if they didn't give me a better life. You created me for an abundant life, and your law contributes to that freedom and abundance.

A TEACHING EXAMPLE

*Be an example to them by doing good works of every kind.
Let everything you do reflect the integrity and seriousness
of your teaching.*

TITUS 2:7 NCV

Being a leader means having a constant audience. People
are always watching to see if you will actually live out what
you teach. It's never easy to live while being held up to a high
standard, but it's worth it to set an example for your students.
When you consistently walk in humility, pointing them back to
God, he will give you the strength to set the example of a life
given to his leadership.

We have to take what we teach seriously. We are not just
teaching academics; we are teaching life: how not to react in
anger, how to make a decision based on wisdom. Even though
we cannot always talk about God in our classrooms, we can
live his gospel in the way we are patient, in the way we show
kindness, in the way we speak with wisdom. Be encouraged
that God will be your source and lead the way for you.

**God, give me the integrity and consistency in my walk with
you to lead by example. Give me the grace and strength to
walk worthy of this position of leadership that I'm in.**

LOVE KNOWS WHAT'S COMING

Be truly glad! There is wonderful joy ahead.... You love him even though you have never seen him. Though you do not see him now, you trust him; and you rejoice with a glorious, inexpressible joy.

1 PETER 1:6, 8–9 NLT

We can be short sighted. We think about what is right in front of us. When we give our lives to Jesus and unlock our faith in him, our sight is instantly expanded. We begin to see so much further than what is right in front of us. We become people of eternity with a future and a hope that is beyond anything we can see.

Stop and think about the reality of eternity. Think about heaven and what waits for you there. Dwell on his promise, his goodness, and his salvation. When you look ahead to what it will be like to finally be in his presence, you can't help but be overcome with joy and hope. There is no fear in love, because love knows what's coming. Love knows the triumph of eternity in his presence. Live a life rejoicing, knowing that everything you've longed for will be realized.

Lord God, thank you for your love. Thank you for the promise of eternity and knowing that even though I can't see you now, I will be with you forever.

BENEFIT OF KINDNESS

Those who are kind benefit themselves.

PROVERBS 11:17 NIV

Kindness is one of the easiest things we can give to another person, and it can make one of the strongest impacts. We were created for relationship. When others, even strangers, treat us unkindly, we feel the sting of that deeply. When we are shown a smile, told a kind word, or given preference, it elevates our hearts and brightens our entire day. We feel valued and loved.

Kindness isn't a favor given away as we often think of it. It is actually a benefit to the one extending it. Being rude and unkind is a disease; it is an attitude that eats at you from the inside out. Unkindness becomes a state of mind and traps you in a place of negativity that quickly transfers from criticism of others into dissatisfaction with yourself. When you love others and are kind to them, you find your own heart being edified. You become a happier, more pleasant person who enjoys life and enjoys those around you.

Lord, make me kind. Let others know that they can come to me for encouragement to feel your love.

MERCIFUL KINDNESS

For His merciful kindness is great toward us,
*And the truth of the L*ORD *endures forever.*
*Praise the L*ORD*!*

PSALM 117:2 NKJV

We are not immune to mistakes. Have you ever done something that made you feel like you couldn't face the Lord? You knew you had let him down and you couldn't bear to stand before him in your failing. Maybe you lost your temper with your students, or your children. Maybe you fell back into that sin you had been victorious over. Perhaps you haven't communicated with him in a long time. You've forgotten how to simply step into his presence.

God's merciful kindness is great toward you. The truth of that statement will never change. He will always forgive you. He will always love you. He will always deal with you kindly. You can be certain of this. No matter what you have done, he will have mercy on you. Be encouraged, today, to admit your mistakes and accept his enduring forgiveness.

God, I need you. I need your mercy. I need your kindness. Thank you for always being gracious to me. Thank you that I don't need to fear your presence, I long for it. When condemnation and fear come over me, remind me of your grace.

LOVE LEARNING

The excellence of knowledge is that wisdom gives life to those who have it.

ECCLESIASTES 7:12 NKJV

If you can teach students to love learning, they will be able to do anything. They will be humble, teachable, and ready to admit their mistakes. The foolish person can't be taught. He believes he already knows everything and his satisfaction with that will keep him from growing. He can't be taught because he will not learn. He can't succeed because he does not believe he fails.

Wise students will never stop learning. They will look to be taught in every situation and they will crave understanding. As they learn, they will grow, and as they grow, they will change themselves and the world around them. They are inventors, innovators, movers, and shakers. They are the ones that will lead revolutions, that will spark revival, and that will raise the next generation of leaders. Teach your students to desire wisdom.

God, I want to teach a classroom full of students who love learning. I know that I need to be teachable as well. I need to be open to rebuke and to be hungry for knowledge. Inspire my mind to learn so I can become a better teacher.

DISCERNING HEART

The heart of the discerning acquires knowledge;
the ears of the wise seek it out.

PROVERBS 18:15 NIV

A fool can't learn from a wise man, but a wise man can learn from a fool. We've all sat in sermons or lectures and listened to a speaker we didn't love. Maybe their facts were off, or they were less than eloquent in their delivery. But a characteristic of a wise man is to seek out knowledge and wisdom even when it's hard to find.

It takes work to chew the meat and spit out the bones. It takes effort to discern the truth from falsehood. When you long to grow in wisdom, you train yourself to learn from anyone in any situation. With the help of the Spirit, your heart will determine what is right. You will accept truth and reject a lie without becoming frustrated with the speaker. You will give grace while humbling yourself to learn. Don't ignore the teachings of someone who is less seasoned. You might miss out on some of the greatest lessons.

God, give me an ear that is teachable and a mind that is discerning. I want to be open to learn from anyone, but wise enough to know what to accept and what to reject. Thank you for giving me your Spirit, who helps me make that choice.

NON-QUARRELSOME CORRECTION

The Lord's servant must not be quarrelsome but kind to everyone, able to teach, patiently enduring evil, correcting his opponents with gentleness.

2 TIMOTHY 2:24-25 ESV

Have you ever met someone who was quick to argue? It feels like they are ready to disagree with everything you say. They look for the opportunity to contradict and instead of correcting in love, they belittle.

It is important to teach others by sharing our wisdom and experiences with them. When you come in contact with those who are wrong or have been misled, it is important to correct them. But *how* you correct them is the most important piece. Have grace for their mistake and gently restore them to the truth. Without patience and gentleness, you will not be convincing.

God, give me the patience to teach others without arguing. Help me to be gentle in my response to those who argue, and to be patient even when I feel frustrated. I am your servant and I want to represent you well.

GOD MOMENTS

Be careful, and watch yourselves closely so that you do not forget the things your eyes have seen or let them fade from your heart as long as you live. Teach them to your children and to their children after them.

DEUTERONOMY 4:9 NIV

There are moments in your life that you can point to and say with absolutely certainty "that was God!" Think about the miracles, or the moments where you were at the end of yourself and you knew it was only Jesus that kept you going. His presence was unexplainable, you felt his hand on you, or you were overcome with peace in a time that should have been full of turmoil.

The power of God is displayed in our testimonies. When we share with our students, our children, and our friends what he has done for us, it allows them to experience the power that we have encountered. It takes that glorious act of God and expands its impact. Run through those moments again in your mind. Encourage others with what God has done for you, and what he is capable of doing for them. Don't let the power of your testimonies fade.

God, thank you for what you have done for me. I owe you my life. I want to speak to everyone about what you've done so they can know that you are faithful.

THE MOST IMPORTANT THING

Always remember what you have been taught,
and don't let go of it.
Keep all that you have learned;
it is the most important thing in life.

PROVERBS 4:13 NCV

Knowledge is a gift. What we've learned throughout our lives has created who we each are today. Our individual experiences, lessons, and moments all make us unique and valuable to the kingdom of God.

Life tries to rob us of what we know of God. We question him when tragedies come, and we turn on him when we've lost our way. When things get really hard, we must hold on to what we know is true. The faithfulness of God. The hope of his glory. The love of a Savior who gave his all. Nothing else in life can save us: nothing but his love, his sacrifice, and his faithfulness. Hold on tightly to what you know. It will keep you afloat in your hardest moments, and it will be your joy and your life forever.

Lord, thank you for what you've taught me. Help me to teach my students how valuable their knowledge is to them. Help me to lead them in truth so what they know can give life to their souls.

SATISFIED SOULS

Satisfy us in the morning with your unfailing love,
that we may sing for joy and be glad all our days.
PSALM 90:14 NIV

Early morning sun streamed in the window. The steam from her coffee cup caught the light on its way upward. Peace settled in as she whispered a soft, "Good morning, Lord." These quiet moments of solitude in his presence were her strength. The pause, the simple escape from the fast pace that defined the rest of her days, was life giving to her. She turned the soft pages in the well-worn Bible and read the words that would keep her going for whatever was ahead of her that day.

Do you take time to satisfy your soul in his presence? We all have different times of the day that we open the Word, but there's something about the morning, something about giving him the first minutes of our day. It's like dedicating your day to him and putting it safely in his hands. If you start your day with the presence of the Lord, you'll find a joy that keeps you singing in the hard moments and peace that settles the worries.

Turn my heart to you, Lord, first thing. Let me think about you when I wake up before I think of anything else.

TEACH WITH YOUR LIFE

Teach these things and insist that everyone learn them....
Be an example to all believers in what you say, in the way
you live, in your love, your faith, and your purity.
1 TIMOTHY 4:11-12 NLT

Being an example is a full-time job. It means teaching with
your life, not just your words. To teach with words requires a
time set aside for teaching that ends when the lesson is done.
To be a true example, however, requires you to teach with your
life by making a commitment to never clock out. It means to
be keenly aware of what impression you are making with the
things you say, the places you go, and the attitude you display.

When you teach about integrity, about value, and about
being kind, you have to back it up with a lifestyle that matches
your teaching. You can't teach your students about patience
while getting frustrated at them when they are slow to
understand. You must be aware of the example you are setting
and the eyes that are watching. Inspire your students to be
loving, kind, pure, and faithful. Make an impact on them that
will last well beyond the lecture.

God, give me the strength to be a consistent and good
example. I don't want to just speak about what I am
teaching; I want to actually live it.

RECEIVE HIS PROMISE

Be like those who through faith and patience will receive what God has promised.

HEBREWS 6:12 NCV

It's easy to become disenchanted with hard work, but God rewards those who serve him diligently. To teach is to make an eternal investment in the kingdom of God, and that alone makes it valuable to him. Don't let the hard days, or the unrewarding moments stop you from pressing on. Remind yourself why you started, re-cast the vision, and keep going.

To persevere requires faith in Jesus and what he has promised to you. It takes patience for the times when you feel like giving up. God will be your strength because he is honored in your work. He will keep you going when you are exhausted, and he will lift you up when you feel hidden. Rest in his promise and remember that your reward is coming. It will be worth every hard minute.

Thank you, God, that you've promised eternal life and reward to those who persevere. Teaching is hard, and it can be thankless, but I know that you value the investment I'm making in the lives of my students. I ask that you would strengthen me for the task.

JOYFUL OBEDIENCE

Great peace have those who love your law,
and nothing can make them stumble.

PSALM 119:165 NIV

There is a huge difference between obligatory obedience and delighted compliance. Perhaps the greatest thing that sets these two apart is a love for the lawgiver. When children love their parents and understand that they only want what is best for them, they obey without question. They aren't concerned whether or not the direction is the right one; they are only concerned with following it.

When you love the Lord and trust the laws laid out for you in his Word, you will have total peace about following them. If you are obeying God simply because you feel you have to, you may question if it's worth it. You have to allow yourself to fall so deeply in love with God that it doesn't even occur to you to go against his law. Children in love with their parents will happily do their bidding because it will be enough for them to know that following the command will bring joy.

God, give me the kind of heart that obeys simply because I want to bring you joy. I desire the kind of peace that comes with unwavering obedience.

A HEART FORMED

May the Lord direct your hearts into God's love and Christ's perseverance.

2 THESSALONIANS 3:5 NIV

Our hearts are easily misled. We are emotional creatures, compelled by our desires and our fears. Too often, we take our eyes off God and place them on the things that we think will satisfy us. Our hearts were created for the perfect love of God, and this world can bring us nowhere near the satisfaction of his love.

When you give your heart to God—the heart he so lovingly formed and created in his image—he will lead you into the pure romance it was created for. There you will find the perseverance you need to resist the false loves of this age and remain hidden in the heart of the Father. Don't become distracted by temptation; keep your heart steady in his hands.

God, hold the gaze of my heart. Don't let me be distracted by sin or evil. I want to have a pure heart that is fixated on you. I want to persevere so that I will receive the reward of being with you forever.

THE ADVOCATE

"The Advocate, the Holy Spirit, whom the Father will send in my name, will teach you all things and will remind you of everything I have said to you."

JOHN 14:26 NIV

When life comes down hard and you feel like you can't breathe against the pressures of it, he's your strength. When you question your decisions and you second-guess your own direction, he's the whisper in your ear telling you which way to turn. When you forget the truth and begin to doubt the promises, the goodness, and the grace, he's your reminder. When you crumble in sadness and break in tragedy, he's your comforter.

The Holy Spirit is the living, breathing presence of Jesus in us. He's the teacher: the one who reminds us what we've learned, who tells us how to obey and walk closely with the Father. He is on our side; his conviction is for our good and his discipline is for our favor. Follow where he moves, and lean into his leading.

Breathe your presence on me, Holy Spirit. Let me feel your Spirit leading me. Thank you for your comfort, for your teaching, for your conviction. Grant me the grace to walk in your light.

I WILL LOOK UP

My voice you shall hear in the morning, O LORD;
In the morning I will direct it to You,
And I will look up.

PSALM 5:3 NKJV

Have you ever stood in the middle of a thick forest, with dense evergreens on all sides and a rich carpet of coppery pine needles? As you look around, all you can see is trees. There is no glimpse of what is beyond them, just dark layers of pine. But if you stop for a moment, and look up to the place where the trees narrow and the light breaks, you are profoundly reminded of how much more is out there. It doesn't matter how hidden you are, there is a big sky and a great God who is always there.

Let the Lord stop you right in the middle of your life. If you find yourself looking around frantically, focusing in on the trials that you can't see past, you will lose sight of what is outside of them. Stop, and look up. Let your eyes adjust and take in the light. Drink in his presence. When you wake up in the morning, before walking forward, before weaving your way through whatever the day might bring, look to his light and speak of his goodness.

Thank you, Jesus, that it is as simple as looking up. Remind me that I'm not alone and that no matter how thick the troubles might stand around me, you are with me and you are guiding me.

TESTED PROMISES

Your promises have been thoroughly tested,
and your servant loves them.
My eyes stay open through the watches of the night
that I may meditate on your promises.

PSALM 119:140, 148 NIV

When we read the promises of God, they can almost become trite. We hear them so often: they are repeated when we are struggling and when we are doing well. We can realize the power of these words in a fresh way when we stop and notice his promises. God promises faithfulness, prosperity, and eternity. And his promises aren't unproven. They are age-old, time-tested promises.

When you lay awake at night and the darkness settles, and your mind turns to the effortless thoughts of fear and anxiety, train your mind to wander to grace. Direct it back to the glory of the Lord and his plans for your precious life. Think about his promises and dwell on them, reminding yourself that they are for you.

God, bring your goodness to my mind. Instead of letting my mind wander to stress and fear and trouble, let my mind wander to you. Be my delight, Lord.

GOOD AND PERFECT GIFTS

Every good gift and every perfect gift is from above, and comes down from the Father of lights, with whom there is no variation or shadow of turning.

JAMES 1:17 NKJV

We sometimes buy into a lie that good things aren't meant for us. We believe we should live a life of suffering for the sake of the gospel, and in some ways that can be true. But God is also your Father who delights in giving you good and perfect gifts. He longs to show you his favor because he loves you and cherishes you.

When God gives a gift, it comes without fine print. He gives generously and freely. There is no variation in his generosity; he doesn't regret his gifts or revoke them. When God gives you a gift, receive it with joy. Thank him for what he has done for you and give him glory when others notice what you have been given.

Thank you, Lord, for the good gifts you give to me. Thank you that your gifts and your love are not dependent on my actions. Your gifts are simply an extension of your unfailing love for me.

INVESTING IN OTHERS

Do nothing out of selfish ambition or vain conceit. Rather, in humility value others above yourselves, not looking to your own interests but each of you to the interests of the others.
PHILIPPIANS 2:3-4 NIV

A beautiful thing happens when we shift our mentality to value others above ourselves. Rather than pushing ahead of those around us in a constant effort to be elevated, we are stretching out our hands to hold theirs and move them forward.

Selfishness is a dangerous path that will only lead to bitterness, disappointment, and a lack of fulfillment. When we make it our purpose to invest in the interests of others, we'll find our own interests being met simultaneously. That's how the kingdom of God works. By humbling ourselves, we are lifted up. By giving ourselves, we are filled. It's the beautiful, nonsensical life of faith. Trust God to meet your needs while you graciously meet the needs of others.

Thank you, God, for setting up a kingdom system that is so far above our earthly one. When you show me grace, it plants a deep desire in me to extend the same. When you meet my needs, I find myself hungry to do the same for others. Your goodness is contagious, and I'm so blessed to be able to both give and receive it.

WORK OF THE LORD

Always give yourselves fully to the work of the Lord,
because you know that your labor in the Lord is not in vain.
1 CORINTHIANS 15:58 NIV

There is a lot in this world that compete for our attention. With so many options of things to give our efforts to, it can be hard to know how much to invest in each demand. As confused as we feel, the honest answer is that God's work is always worthy of giving everything to. Anything else is temporary.

With so many good commitments available, how do we truly know what is God-ordained for us? We look to him. We seek his guidance. We ask him to open the doors he wants us to walk through and to close the ones that aren't of him. We evaluate every opportunity and ask ourselves if it's in line with his kingdom standards. We seek his face, read his Word, and trust that he'll make it clear to us. And once he has, we pour ourselves into what he has set before us, knowing with confidence that it will be eternally worth all our sacrifice and efforts.

God, show me clearly what your work for me is. I want to bring honor to you and be an effective participant in your kingdom. Thank you for using me.

SERVANT TO ALL

Though I am free from all, I have made myself
a servant to all, that I might win more of them.
1 CORINTHIANS 9:19 ESV

When we give our lives to Christ, we free ourselves from the lure of the world. Our obligations lie only with our heavenly Father. When we give of ourselves to others, without owing them anything, we advance the kingdom of God. We show the sacrificial love of Christ that wasn't owed but was freely given.

Our goal on this earth is to be the visible expression of the invisible God. We are his ambassadors, showing the world his love for them. By choosing to serve those we are not obligated to, we will win their hearts for God. The world is accustomed to a love that is tainted; an affection that comes with rules, conditions, and selfishness. When you demonstrate the pure love of the Father that is abundant even when it isn't returned, hearts will be softened and changed.

Lord, make me a servant of others. Give me a heart that is ready and willing to give. Make me consistent in your love so my expression of it can be pure.

POSITION OF SERVICE

"If I then, your Lord and Teacher, have washed your feet, you also ought to wash one another's feet."
JOHN 13:14 NKJV

Imagine how it must have felt in the room when Jesus washed the disciples' feet. Here was the man they had followed. The one they looked up to as he addressed crowds of thousands. The one they had watched live in perfection, always speaking right to their soul. The admiration they had for him was unmatched. They had come to view him as their friend, leader, and Lord. But when he knelt down, untied their sandals, and washed their feet, they must have felt blown away. Imagine the humility.

In light of that story, how can we not feel compelled to humble ourselves to love others? We need to serve them, to kneel down to meet their needs, to show them preference and value. This position of service is one of honor because it is the position that Jesus took for his followers.

God, I never want to see myself as higher than others. I want to wash the feet of those who I am in leadership over. I want to meet their needs in such a way that I make them feel valued.

COMMIT YOUR WAY

Commit your actions to the LORD,
and your plans will succeed.

PROVERBS 16:3 NLT

We hold tightly to life. We carefully measure our plans and choose our direction. Often, we can see a clear path leading where we want to go and we head down it with excitement and fervor. But when God redirects us, and life knocks us back, it is hard to avoid the feeling of disappointment.

God promises that when we commit our way to him, and trust him with our futures, he will bring success. We may not understand why he is leading us a certain way; it doesn't make sense, so we try to redirect. If you have those doubts today, try to step back and hold your life with open hands. God can do something with your life that is far beyond where you ever would have gone without his leading.

God, you make my path secure. Stop me when I try to control my own plans. I want to be led by you and not by what I think is best. You see the whole picture. I only see what is right ahead. I trust you, Lord, to make beauty out of my life.

SUN BEYOND THE CLOUDS

Enter his gates with thanksgiving,
and his courts with praise!
Give thanks to him; bless his name!
For the LORD is good; his steadfast love endures forever,
and his faithfulness to all generations.

PSALM 100:4-5 ESV

A heart that is thankful welcomes the presence of God. This is a heart that pauses, that appreciates, that wonders. This is the soul that drinks in the simple beauty of his peace, and rests in his reminders.

The most beautiful example you can set for your students is an attitude of thankfulness. Complaint is rampant in our culture. We shift blame and we find fault, and we vent it all to the world. But the brightest light you can shine to the world around you is to give thanks. Let your eyes be opened in gratefulness and find the sun beyond the clouds to see the blessing in each trial.

God, give me a heart that is readily grateful. Let it sing your praise even when complaint is on my lips. Give me a sense of wonder for all your good gifts. Help me to display that to my students so they will also learn to thank you in all things.

DISCIPLINE'S HARVEST

No discipline seems pleasant at the time, but painful. Later on, however, it produces a harvest of righteousness and peace for those who have been trained by it.

HEBREWS 12:11 NIV

The sting of consequence from wrongdoing can leave us feeling empty and full of regret. Discipline may not feel good, but it allows us to stop and recognize our wrongs. Without correction, we could blow through life without learning a single lesson.

Standing on the other side of rebuke, there is always a strengthened heart. He who has been forgiven much loves much, and understands the love of discipline. Have you felt the sting of rebuke lately? Allow yourself to recognize the lesson of righteousness that will develop you into a strong conqueror. When you understand the grace of God and the redemption that he gives, you will no longer dread discipline. Be thankful in the midst of correction as you begin to harvest the benefits of righteousness.

God, I don't look with anticipation for your discipline, but I know that you discipline the ones you love, and I am so thankful for that affection. Grow me daily into a person you can use.

TELL THE STORIES

I will teach you hidden lessons from our past—
stories we have heard and known,
stories our ancestors handed down to us.
We will not hide these truths from our children;
we will tell the next generation
about the glorious deeds of the LORD,
about his power and his mighty wonders.

PSALM 78:2-4 NLT

Nothing quite matches the intensity of seeing God work. We see him in miracles, in a life changed, in a situation reversed. All are witnesses to the acts of God. It is encouraging to hear of these powerful moments firsthand. We hear the passion expressed in the inflection of a voice, the brightness of eyes as memories are recalled, and the smile on a face as miracles are conveyed.

The great legacy of faith that we have in Christ is passed down through our testimony. It's continued through the sharing of stories and memories. Teach your students about what God has done in your life. If you can't say it outright, tell it in a story. Proclaim God's greatness through your experiences, and let his Spirit do the rest of the work.

Thank you, Jesus, for your acts of power throughout history. Help me to tell your story and to teach future generations what you have done in my life.

WALK IN TRUTH

I have no greater joy than to hear that my children
are walking in the truth.
3 JOHN 1:4 NIV

The truth sets us free. We know that, but we complicate it. We try to hide things, to cover up and paint ourselves in the best light. Having to cover things is not freedom. True freedom is found in the ability to lay everything bare before a gracious God and trust that he understands and forgives. Truth allows us to walk in love with others who have also been known and forgiven.

Truth isn't something to be afraid of; it's something to embrace. Darkness does not survive when the truth shines on it. When everything is exposed and everything is known, we can stand tall with no need to hide. Our freedom comes from being fully known and fully loved.

Heavenly Father, I've spent so much time and energy trying to hide things from you. Help me to understand that you fully know me and yet you still love me. Let me be so confident in your love and so desperate for your grace that I hold nothing back.

WORTH A PROMISE

The Lord always keeps his promises;
he is gracious in all he does.
PSALM 145:13 NLT

Remember being a child and how much a promise was worth? We'd reach for the hand of our best friend, clench it tightly, and with a sober expression we'd swear our allegiance to one another. As we grew older, we found that a promise was worth a little less than we'd thought. We grew to find that changes come, emotions shift, and circumstances arise.

People will come into your life on the heels of broken promises. They will have, at some time in their life, felt let down. You can't change the past or repair their lost hopes. But what you can do is point them to the only person that will keep every promise he makes. He is committed to their dreams and supplies them with hope. Teach them about the Father and how gracious he is toward them. He is reliable and faithful, and you can trust in that too.

God, remind me of the weight of a promise. I can trust that your promises will never be broken. In a world of changing minds and human uncertainty, you are my steady place.

DECEMBER

Come, let us
bow down in worship,
let us kneel before
the LORD our Maker.

PSALM 95:6 NIV

WISDOM FROM ABOVE

The wisdom from above is first of all pure. It is also peace loving, gentle at all times, and willing to yield to others. It is full of mercy and good deeds. It shows no favoritism and is always sincere.

JAMES 3:17 NLT

Wisdom isn't always about being right. It is not about a head full of information or correct facts. The characteristics of wisdom are much more than that. Wisdom is pure; it comes from truth and a heart that is right before God. Wisdom is peace and gentleness; it does not start an argument for the sake of winning it or attempt to expose the flaws of others. Wisdom is willing to yield to others because it treasures right relationship and humility before God. Wisdom is merciful. It is confidence that is never threatened and doesn't need to be proven. Wisdom doesn't favor anyone; it is fair. Wisdom speaks the truth, and gives credit where credit is due.

Seek wisdom from God. Ask him to give it to you generously.

Lord God, I need your wisdom. I have young minds that listen to what I have to say and that watch how I enter conversations. I want to show them what it looks like to have wisdom from above. Grant me the kind of wisdom that points only to you.

WEIGHT OF WORRY

Worry weighs a person down;
an encouraging word cheers a person up.
PROVERBS 12:25 NLT

How many hours of our lives have we wasted on empty worry? How many happy moments have we let pass by because we allowed anxiety to shadow our joy? Troubles will come; they are inevitable. But what is, is. We can't change a thing by dwelling on what could be or what might happen.

When worries creep in, dwell on the words of God and the promises he gives. Encourage those around you, especially those who are caught in worry. Remind them of his faithfulness. Let it fill you so full of expectation and hope that anxiety has no place to gain hold. God sees everything and knows all the possibilities. Take courage in his control and let go of the weight of worry that holds you back from freedom.

Jesus, I don't want to worry anymore. I want to live a fearless life in your joy and your peace. I'm so thankful for your love and encouragement. Let me be an encouragement to others, helping to free them from fear and worry.

FACED WITH LOVE

If we are faithless, he remains faithful—
for he cannot deny himself.

2 TIMOTHY 2:13 ESV

We expect to be matched in relationship. Our misguided sense of justice believes that love takes two. We think that whatever effort we put into our relationship with God will define its passion. But God always gives us everything. We can hold back from him, but he does not hold back from us. He already gave everything up. His love cannot be diluted—not even by our apathy.

When we turn our back on God, he is still facing us. When we wander to another lover, he moves toward us, ready for our return. He is faithful and true and nothing will ever change that. His faithfulness is his definition. It doesn't matter how far you have wandered, or what other loves you have entertained, he will forever be facing you with love.

God, I'm humbled by your faithfulness to me. Show me when I believe the lie that my unfaithfulness affects your love. Thank you that you have never wavered. Your face is toward me, nudging my heart and pursuing my soul. Teach me to walk faithfully in you.

HEALING THROUGH JESUS

Jesus was going throughout all Galilee, teaching in their synagogues and proclaiming the gospel of the kingdom, and healing every kind of disease and every kind of sickness among the people.

MATTHEW 4:23 NASB

It is hard to understand how and when God heals his children. Have you prayed for healing recently and haven't got any better? Are there students in your class that are unwell and not recovering? It can be disheartening when you are sick, or see others that you care about not improving.

Our faith does not need to be great, but through our belief in Jesus, we can also acknowledge our belief in the miracles that he performed. Jesus showed us that what we think is impossible is not impossible with God.

God, when healing doesn't come, I trust that you are still faithful and gracious. Let me be encouraged today to believe that you will bring healing to the sick. Bless the children in my care and bring them full health.

LIVING WORD

The word of God is living and active and sharper than any two-edged sword, and piercing as far as the division of soul and spirit, of both joints and marrow, and able to judge the thoughts and intentions of the heart.

HEBREWS 4:12 NASB

Sometimes God speaks in themes. We all go through different seasons in life, and God speaks to our hearts accordingly. Some of us may be going through a season of learning to wait, while others are learning how to step out in faith. The beautiful thing about God is that he is big enough to speak to all of us—in our different places, with our different hearts—at the same time, with the same words.

God's Word is alive and active. It can deliver truth to the heart of each person. Two people can get something completely different from the same passage of Scripture because of what God has been doing in each of their hearts separately. Share what God is teaching you with your students. It can speak to all of them right where they are.

God, help me not to doubt the power of what your Word. You know me so intimately because you are the one who handcrafted my soul. Thank you for caring enough to speak directly to my heart through your living Word.

EXERCISING SELF-CONTROL

So think clearly and exercise self-control. Look forward to the gracious salvation that will come to you when Jesus Christ is revealed to the world.

1 PETER 1:13 NLT

In grade school, we had to wait to speak until our hand was raised. The teacher would not call on a single student until she had finished talking. The children could barely wait another second before blurting out the answer. These teachers were wise. They were trying to teach self-control—a valuable life lesson.

Lack of self-control comes in a variety of forms: overeating, spending too much time on the computer or phone, losing our tempers, wasting money, gossiping, and the list goes on. Self-control requires discipline. In order to perfect it, we need to practice and ask God for help.

God, help me to show self-control at work and at home. Give me grace and patience to teach the children you have placed in my care. Let them learn self-control because they see it in me.

PEACE LIKE A RIVER

"I am the LORD your God,
who teaches you what is best for you,
who directs you in the way you should go
…your peace would have been like a river,
your well-being like the waves of the sea."

ISAIAH 48:17-18 NIV

Where do you usually go to find peace? Is there a certain place? A certain person? One of the greatest gifts of God is his undeniable, unfathomable peace. It is a deep well that comes with knowing and experiencing Jesus' love. No matter where we are, where we are going, and whatever we might be experiencing, his peace is greater.

Grasp how deep his well runs. Lasting peace and joy do not come in the world or people around you. Although those can be comforting, true, transforming, and powerful peace can only come from our Father. And oh, how he loves when we come to his well.

God, thank you for teaching me what is best for me. Thank you for your peace that is like a river; it washes over me and directs me in the way I should go.

HIDDEN BLESSINGS

"They are blessed who grieve, for God will comfort them."
MATTHEW 5:4 NCV

There are hidden blessings to be found in the midst of our troubles. One of them is that we are better able to care for others and to show compassion when we have been there ourselves. God is the source of all comfort, and he teaches us this gift as well.

The Lord shows us mercy and gives us peace that passes understanding even in the middle of our greatest pain. Because of this, when others are troubled and struggling, we have learned the true meaning of comfort and we're able to pass it along.

God, I know that some of the students in my class are hurting. Help me to be compassionate and caring, and to direct them to you to find comfort.

STORYTELLING

"I will talk in parables; I will explain mysteries hidden since the beginning of time."
MATTHEW 13:34 TLB

We enjoy listening to stories because they help us relate with a concept and personalize an idea. We hear a lofty explanation and struggle to understand, but a story illustrates the same thought and we become connected to it.

Jesus was a storyteller. While he walked the earth, he told people many stories in order to teach them something. Jesus used parables and imagery instead of "just spitting it out" so people would meditate, speculate, study, and absorb the words to better understand them. The parables that Jesus told weren't just simple stories; their symbolisms revealed secrets of the kingdom of heaven and made its glory digestible for the common man.

God, help me to share my stories of your work in my life with the students in my class. I know it will help open their hearts and minds to you if they can connect your love with something tangible. Please give me the right words to share at the right time.

FOOLISH WISDOM

"I will destroy the wisdom of the wise; the intelligence of the intelligent I will frustrate." Where is the wise person? Where is the teacher of the law? Where is the philosopher of this age? Has not God made foolish the wisdom of the world?

1 CORINTHIANS 1:19-20 NIV

Our culture today is one that values intelligence and an educated mind; philosophers and the great thinkers are among the highly esteemed. It can be easy to get caught up (or left behind!) in debates of religion, politics, and philosophy. The problem with worldly wisdom is that it is self-generated; it exists in the context of a finite mind that cannot grasp the mysteries of God.

When Jesus came into the world, whom did he upset the most? That's right, the Scribes and the Pharisees—the most learned people of that time. He turned their ideas and assumptions upside-down and frustrated their intelligence. God's wisdom is for those who are humble enough to accept his ways. This is how he makes the foolish wise.

Father, when I feel like I am unable to answer the intellectual bullies around me, help me to look at the source of their wisdom. I only want to trust in your wisdom that is eternal and life-giving.

ALL OF YOU

One of them, an expert in the law, tested him with this question: "Teacher, which is the greatest commandment in the Law?" Jesus replied: "'Love the Lord your God with all your heart and with all your soul and with all your mind.' This is the first and greatest commandment."

MATTHEW 22:34-38 NIV

The Pharisees were always trying to trip up Jesus. They wanted nothing more than to find fault with him—a reason to put him on trial or do away with him. So when they asked him which of all the commandments was the greatest, they were hoping that he would somehow fail to come up with the correct answer. Instead, as usual, he got it right. And, oh, how right it was! When we love the Lord our God with all our hearts, everything else falls into place.

Put God first in your heart and life. Then, when students test you with myriads of questions, you can trust God to give you the right answer at just the right time.

God, I want to give you all of me. I want to love you with all of my heart, soul, and mind. Crumble all the walls around my heart so I can love you fully today.

RISK

The LORD is my light and my salvation; whom shall I fear?
The LORD is the stronghold of my life;
of whom shall I be afraid?

PSALM 27:1 ESV

Most great things in life take some risk. We probably can each say that we've taken some pretty dumb chances in life, but we have also taken some incredible ones. Some of our risks end in disaster, but others in sheer beauty.

One thing all risk has in common is that it teaches something. We never walk away unchanged. And while stepping out and taking the risk itself is scary, we discover our own bravery in it. Trusting God requires our faith, which is a risk. But taking a risk is necessary to follow God wholeheartedly. Of course, it's easier to sit on the sidelines. To slide under the radar. To live safe. But letting fear hold us back from taking a risk keeps us from the breathtaking possibilities of life.

Father, I know sometimes I need to jump. I want to set aside my own understanding of situations and trust what you are saying to me. I know the kind of risk required for faith in you is the kind with the greatest reward.

HERO

Grace to you and peace from God our Father and the Lord Jesus Christ, who gave Himself for our sins so that He might rescue us from this present evil age, according to the will of our God and Father, to whom be the glory forevermore.

GALATIANS 1:3-5 NIV

When Jesus came down from sitting at the right hand of the Father as the Savior of the world, it was a rescue mission. He came down, in love, and rescued us. He delivered us from our sin. We are forever his. And we are forever freed. There is no other love that loves without borders. And it is free. Let that resonate in your heart. He came down in love and rescued you…for free.

Jesus truly is the hero in our fairy tale. No matter what we experience today, we should let that sink in.

Father, I don't want to doubt the love you have for me. Let this truth sink deep into my heart. I have been rescued by you, and your love for me is without boundary. Thank you.

LOVE WELL

Follow God's example, therefore, as dearly loved children and walk in the way of love, just as Christ loved us and gave himself up for us as a fragrant offering and sacrifice to God.
EPHESIANS 5:1-2 NIV

If we do anything right, let it be that we love well. Loving well looks different for each person, but we know it when we do it: when we love whole-heartedly. We can't change the entire world—only Jesus can do that—but we can change the world for one person. One student. One class.

There are big things you can do to love well, but loving well can be done in little, everyday moments too. We love despite feelings. We love when it's tough. We love when we don't necessarily want to. We love well because we are called to: because God loved us first.

God, help me to love the way you do. It is easy to say but so hard to do. I desire to love each student in my class well, and I need your help to carry it out.

THE CALL FOR HELP

> I look up to the hills,
> but where does my help come from?
> My help comes from the LORD,
> who made heaven and earth.
>
> PSALM 121:1-2 NCV

Depending on the type of person you are, you may not be very good at asking for help. There are those who like to be the helpers: they do best serving others because they feel capable and useful. Then there are those who gladly accept service any time they are given the opportunity. Neither is better than the other, and both have their positive elements.

In different seasons of life, natural helpers may need to be the ones receiving help. As teachers, this can be hard to accept, and we have to be careful not to let pride take control. Asking for help is part of being vulnerable: we push everything aside to say, "I can't do this alone." God has put people in our lives who love to help, but they won't know we need it until we ask. Sometimes those helpers are found right in your classroom. Let them help you.

God, help me to take a chance on the people you have intricately placed in my life. I know there are those who love to help and it's important for me to admit that I need them. Give me grace to ask for help.

DO YOU REALLY NEED IT?

Be rich in good works and give happily to those in need,
always being ready to share with others whatever
God has given.

1 TIMOTHY 6:18 TLB

Christmastime is a wonderful time, full of celebration and goodwill. So it seems right to get into the spirit of Christmas and gift-giving. Most of us love the opportunity to shop until late, buy good gifts for our friends and family, and maybe even splurge a little on ourselves.

Generosity is a wonderful thing to exhibit during the Christmas season, but let's not confuse giving with spending. Spending will not give you joy; giving your money to bless others and do good will.

God, gifts are wonderful, but I want to dwell on the goodness that I can share with others, especially those in need. Show me how to do that this Christmas season.

CLAY

Now, O Lord, you are our Father;
we are the clay, and you are our potter;
we are all the work of your hand.

ISAIAH 64:8 ESV

Life can be busy. Whatever season you are in, there are always things to be done. More often than not, our wellbeing is cast aside because of all the other things that need to be tended to. Our Creator says that we are jars of clay. If left out and not tended to, that jar of clay can dry out and crack.

If we can give God our obedience and our time, he promises us his abundance and peace, quenching our very driest parts. Oh, the renewal we receive when we sit in his presence, letting him fill our spirit with his love and gentle, encouraging words!

God, I feel most renewed when I spend time in your presence. I ask for your peace to fill my soul and spill out to those around me. Refresh me in your Word as I spend some quiet time with you.

LET GOD WIN

Truthful words stand the test of time,
but lies are soon exposed.

PROVERBS 12:19 NLT

Don't believe the lies. There is an enemy out there who wants to steal, kill, and destroy. One of the most powerful ways he does that is through filling our hearts with things we think are true about ourselves. Those lies fill our minds with hatred, so that when we look in the mirror, we start hating what we see. *I'm so ugly. I don't deserve anything good in my life. I screwed up again. Why do I even try?*

These thoughts are not from God. He loves us! He knits us together and sets us apart. He cherishes every breath we take, and in the name of Jesus, we can rebuke the enemy so those lies no longer fill our heads and overtake our hearts.

Jesus, lift the veil from my eyes so I can see clearly. Thank you that you would move mountains for me. Help me to know your love so deeply that I can't help but share its truth with others.

CYCLE

To the praise of the glory of His grace, which He freely bestowed on us in the Beloved. In Him we have redemption through His blood, the forgiveness of our trespasses, according to the riches of His grace which He lavished on us.

EPHESIANS 1:6-8 NASB

Have you ever said or done something that you immediately regretted? It just happened: that horrible moment you replay over and over again. Then, maybe a few days later, something similar happens. Why does this happen? Why can't we exercise more self-control?

Those moments are the vicious cycle of our humanness. Thankfully, through the blood of Jesus Christ and our repentance, we are forgiven, set free, and released of the burden of our mistakes. We are given a clean slate to start over. And some days that gift feels bigger than others. Sometimes we rely heavily on the grace of our Lord just to get through the day. And that is okay.

Jesus, thank you for your forgiveness. You wipe my slate clean and let me start over. Help me practice this same forgiveness with my family, my students, my friends, and my enemies. God, I desperately need your grace every day.

CHASE WISDOM

Teach the wise, and they will become even wiser;
teach good people, and they will learn even more.
PROVERBS 9:9 NCV

The moment a person decides they can't learn anything from someone is the moment they stop learning at all. It is openness to being taught that makes a man wise. The wisest people never stop learning, never stop exploring, seeing, or doing. They have an insatiable hunger to be taught. They understand that they are not the experts on everything and that there is always a person with more experience, more knowledge, and more passion.

Never close yourself off to learning something new—not even from your students. In their moments of frustration or failure, you can learn. You can learn to lead them better. You can learn to love them well. You can learn from their exploration and their eagerness. You can learn from their triumph and their celebration. You can learn to stop putting pressure on yourself, and instead rejoice in lifelong education. Chase wisdom—never arrive at it.

Teach me daily, Lord. I want to be open to new understanding. Humble my heart so that I can learn from anyone.

THE SELF ELF

*He died for everyone so that those who receive his new life
will no longer live for themselves. Instead, they will live for
Christ, who died and was raised for them.*

2 Corinthians 5:15 NLT

Can we ever truly grasp what Jesus had to give up in order
to become human and walk this earth with us? Scripture tells
us that although Jesus had equality with God, he gave up his
supreme entitlement to become human. We may never quite
understand this act, but I think we can accept that Jesus' birth
and death on the cross was our ultimate example of sacrifice.

We may be involved in the spirit of giving this season, but
are we involved in the spirit of *giving up*? Are we willing to
sacrifice, as in the example of Jesus, regarding others before
ourselves? This is not to attribute a higher worth based on
superior authority or qualities, but to understand people's
value in light of Christ.

**Lord, I recognize that I am prone to selfishness. Thank you
for your sacrifice. Help me to see the good in everyone
around me and pursue their interests above my own. Truly
this is how you lived, and I want to be more like you.**

CHRISTMAS TRUCE

May the Lord of peace Himself give you peace always in every way. The Lord be with you all.

2 THESSALONIANS 3:16 NKJV

In the Christmas of 1914, German and British soldiers declared a Christmas truce and began a series of widespread ceasefires along the Western Front. In the week leading up to the holiday, soldiers crossed trenches and ventured into no man's land to exchange seasonal greetings and food, play football, and take part in joint burial ceremonies and prisoner swaps. The Christmas truce is seen as a symbolic moment of peace and humanity amidst one of the most violent events of human history.

The Christmas spirit is often talked of throughout this season, and while at times it seems to take away from the pure celebration of Christ, it is encouraging to read of stories where goodwill seems to conquer in the midst of a stressful and often hurtful world.

God, even though I might not be able to share your peace freely with my students, I pray that you would help me to create harmony in my classroom. You are more evident in my class than people may realize because you are with me, and that means peace is with me too.

STOP AND LISTEN

Martha was distracted with all her preparations;
and she came up to Him and said, "Lord, do You not care
that my sister has left me to do all the serving alone?
Then tell her to help me." But the Lord answered and
said to her, "Martha, Martha, you are worried and bothered
about so many things; but only one thing is necessary,
for Mary has chosen the good part, which shall not be
taken away from her."

LUKE 10:40-42 NASB

The Bible story of Martha and Mary is well known, and many of us feel rather empathetic toward Martha. As teachers, we manage many responsibilities and tasks, and it requires a lot of hard work and hospitality. This seems especially true as we approach Christmas, when our "to-do" lists grow, and events and celebrations take over our lives.

But sometimes in this season, we worry about the unnecessary things—things that will not last beyond the day. Mary chose the "good part" when Jesus was visiting. She focused on the guest, not the preparations.

Lord, show me what things are distracting me from what really matters. As I take a moment to reflect on you today, let me remember that this is the best part of my day. This is what helps me make it through the rest of the day.

WHAT HE SAYS

*"I am the Lord's servant. May everything you have
said about me come true."*
LUKE 1:38 NLT

In a memorable scene from a movie about teenage girls, a
teacher asks a gymnasium full of young women to close their
eyes and raise their hands if they've ever said anything bad
about another girl. Every hand is raised. The reason this scene
rings true is that it *is* true. And sadly, we are often even harder
on ourselves.

In addition to the amazing news that Mary would bear
God's son, the angel who visits her in Luke 1 also tells Mary of
her goodness, of her favor in God's eyes. Mary was a teenage
girl. Chances are she'd heard—and thought—something
less than kind about herself on more than one occasion. But
consider her brave, beautiful response.

**God, I know I am critical of myself and others. Today I
choose to listen to what you have to say about me. Help
me to hear what you have to say about others as well, so I
can treat them with love and care.**

CARRY THE STORY

*In that region there were shepherds living in the fields,
keeping watch over their flock by night. Then an angel
of the Lord stood before them, and the glory of the
Lord shone around them, and they were terrified.
But the angel said to them, "Do not be afraid; for see—
I am bringing you good news of great joy for all the
people: to you is born this day in the city of David
a Savior, who is the Messiah, the Lord."*

LUKE 2:8-11 NRSV

You will probably celebrate today with some manner of
tradition. We celebrate with popular cultural traditions and
with our own particular family traditions. Whatever these
traditions are, you probably hold them very near to your heart
and hope they will last as time goes on.

Have you ever felt lost in all the tradition and wondered if
Jesus is truly being celebrated? It's easy to feel disappointed
when we forget to elevate Jesus in all of the celebrations.
But remember, our celebration of this day actually serves the
purpose of carrying the story of Good News forward!

**God, help me not to frown on the fact that the world has
commercialized this paramount event in history. Instead,
help me use the festivities to glorify you. Show me people
I can share your story with so it will continue to be told
throughout generations.**

BOXING DAY

All who are under the yoke of slavery should consider their masters worthy of full respect, so that God's name and our teaching may not be slandered.
1 TIMOTHY 6:1 NIV

In many countries around the world, the day after Christmas is called Boxing Day: a tradition that began in a time when tradespeople were given Christmas boxes of money or presents to acknowledge good service throughout the year.

While we don't like to think of ourselves as servants these days, many of us are involved in employment or some type of service—especially teachers! The Bible says much about those that have shown diligence and respect to those who are in authority. There is a higher purpose to us respecting our employers. We may not get our Boxing Day reward for recognition of our service, but we will be honoring God's name as a witness of Christian living.

Lord remind me that as I serve the children in my care, I am positively representing your name and your heart. Give me grace and strength to continue.

HIGHWAYS

"My thoughts are not your thoughts,
nor are your ways my ways, says the LORD.
For as the heavens are higher than the earth,
so are my ways higher than your ways
and my thoughts than your thoughts."

ISAIAH 55:8-9 NRSV

If you stop to think about it, most of our conversations are made up of a dialogue of various opinions. We talk about the facts, for sure, but the meaningful stuff comes when we start to influence those facts with our own sentiments.

There's nothing wrong with searching for meaning in situations and trying to make sense of the complexities of life. It's possible that the quest for understanding is an integral part of our human nature. However, we ultimately need to surrender our understanding and opinions to God's truth.

God, I surrender my ways and thoughts to yours. Thank you that even though I can't always understand your ways, I can trust that they are better.

NEW EVERY MORNING

Because of the Lord's great love, we are not consumed,
for his compassions never fail.
They are new every morning;
great is your faithfulness.

LAMENTATIONS 3:22-23 NIV

Some days it is good to reflect on exactly what God has saved us from. As a nation, Israel knew what it was to fail God time and time again. They rebelled against him and they deserved punishment; yet, God chose to redeem them, over and over again. His love for his people compelled him to show mercy.

We are not unlike the Israelites in our rebellion and turning away from God's purposes. We are also not unlike the Israelites in that God has incredible compassion for us. In sending his Son, Jesus Christ, God proved once and for all that his compassion will never fail.

God, I can't go one day without failing. Thank you for your faithfulness and mercies that are new every morning. I embrace it all today and choose to move forward in forgiveness.

DON'T BE ASHAMED

I am suffering now because I tell the Good News, but I am not ashamed, because I know Jesus, the One in whom I have believed. And I am sure he is able to protect what he has trusted me with until that day.

2 TIMOTHY 1:12 NCV

Have you ever tried to wade upstream through a river, or swim against a strong current? It is hard! Sometimes this is how we feel as Christians in a world full of unbelievers. Our modern culture is full of political correctness and accepting all beliefs, but when it comes to Christianity, it feels like anything we say is offensive!

Paul was put in prison a number of times for offending the people of his time. He seemed to suffer gladly because he was convinced that Jesus was the Savior and that his mission was to share this good news with the world. Paul was convinced of the truth, and because of this, he was not ashamed.

Father God, thank you for the confidence you give me to share my faith with others. I am not ashamed of you. I trust you to protect me as the world becomes more hostile to my belief in you. You are faithful and you are good.

MIND OVER MATTER

Bodily exercise profits a little, but godliness is profitable for all things, having promise of the life that now is and of that which is to come.

1 TIMOTHY 4:8 NKJV

As you look toward the New Year, you will probably think about your goals and aspirations. And one of those goals is likely to exercise more! We know the value of exercise; it benefits the body and the mind. We also know that exercise requires determination and discipline.

There is, however, exercise that is more beneficial than physical exercise. Scripture compares godliness with bodily exercise. Godliness is not just something that we instantly receive when we accept Christ as our Savior. Godliness is a work in progress. It requires discipline and commitment to understanding what it means to be like Jesus.

God, I know that I have to put time and effort into growing my relationship with you. Help me to prioritize godliness above the other distractions in life. I know that I will be rewarded both in this life and eternity when I make you my first priority.

ON THE RIGHT TRACK

"For I know the plans I have for you," declares the LORD,
"plans to prosper you and not to harm you, plans to give
you hope and a future."
JEREMIAH 29:11 NIV

What are you going to do next year? When we are
experiencing the end of one year and looking toward the next,
we can become overwhelmed with the need to plan what we
hope to achieve. Maybe you hope to advance your career, find
a husband, have a child, go on a missions trip, or further your
education.

When your heart motivation for those plans is right, you
need not be anxious about how you are going to make it
happen. The Lord is always present to guide you in the way
you should go. God also knows that plans don't happen
without steps. So before you hit the ground running with your
ideas, allow him to show you the next step.

**Father God, thank you that you don't lead me into anything
you haven't prepared me for. I ask for your guidance in
both my plans for next year and the steps I need to take to
get there. I surrender my ways to yours, knowing that you
know what is best for me.**